Dealing with Death

Look for these and other books in the Lucent Overview series:

AIDS
Dealing with Death
Endangered Species
Garbage
Homeless Children
Smoking
Special Effects in the Movies
Vietnam

Dealing with Death

by Norma Gaffron

LUCENT
B·O·O·K·S

LUCENT *Overview Series*

Lucent Overview Series

Library of Congress Cataloging-in-Publication Data

Gaffron, Norma, 1931-
    Dealing with death / by Norma Gaffron.
        p.   cm. — (Lucent overview series)
    Includes bibliographical references.
    Summary: Explores the biological, emotional, legal, and philosophical aspects of death, including causes of death, cross-cultural perspectives on death and its aftermath, and ways of coping with the deaths of people we know.
    ISBN 1-56006-108-1
    1. Death—Juvenile literature. [1. Death.] I. Title.
II. Series.
HQ1073.3.G34   1989
306.9—dc20   89-37592
                                                                    CIP
                                                                    AC

To all those who shared with me
their feelings about death and dying

Contents

CHAPTER ONE

Facing the Facts About Death

When a group of high school students met to discuss their feelings about death, Ann* said, "My mother talks about death as if it's a secret. She whispers." Some of the other students in the class nodded to show they understood.

Like Ann's mother, many people find it difficult to talk about death. They say the word in the hushed tones we reserve for something we fear. Or they avoid the word entirely. When fifteen-year-old Brian, a victim of leukemia, died, his school principal made this announcement over the intercom: "I'm sorry to have to tell you that Brian passed away early this morning."

"Why didn't you say Brian died?" asked the health teacher whose class had just finished a unit on death.

"I just didn't feel comfortable with that word," the principal replied.

Passed away is not the only term used as a substitute for a word that may offend someone or suggest something unpleasant. We often hear comments such as "She lost her husband." Or, "Our dog was so old and sick the vet put her to sleep." Slang such as "he kicked

---

*Note: The stories in this book are all about real people. In most cases their names are changed or are not used, at their request.

the bucket,'' or ''he bought the farm'' are other ways of avoiding the word. These are all terms people use to protect themselves from the grim realities of death. Doctors call them adjustment mechanisms. They serve an immediate need. As the concept of death becomes less painful, the woman who lost her husband, for instance, may be able to say, ''He died.''

When it comes to our own death, it is even harder to face reality. Sometimes we go so far as to say, ''If I die . . . ,'' when we really mean ''When I die . . . ,'' for we know that everything that lives will someday die.

Why all the secrecy, the hush-hush tones? Dr. Elisabeth Kübler-Ross, well-known authority on death and dying, says death is ''a fearful, frightening happening, and the fear of death is 'a universal fear.''' Because of that, death is a subject that is ''evaded, ignored, and denied.''

But if we continue to try to ignore death, change the subject, and refuse to discuss it because it is morbid, the mystery that surrounds death will only increase our fear. Death is a natural part of the life cycle. Sooner or later, someone close to us will die. Learning about death will make it easier to deal with the feelings and responsibilities that accompany the end of a life. We will be better able to respond to the needs of others and to face the unknown if we have as many facts as possible.

We can begin by seeking an answer to the question, What is death?

Finding a definition

Fairy tale author Hans Christian Andersen often left a note on his bedside table that read, ''I only seem dead.'' He did this because he was terrified of being buried alive. In the past it was not unusual for people to have such fears. Friends rigged up gadgets such as bells or alarms to allow the person who seemed dead to signal from the coffin if he or she woke up. It was common practice for friends and relatives to watch over the body for a day or so, just in case.

Reprinted from *Love Is Hell* by Matt Groening. Courtesy of Pantheon Books, a division of Random House, Inc., NY

Of course doctors had tests for death. They would listen for a heartbeat. If there was none, they held a mirror or a feather up to the person's nose. If the mirror did not fog over or the feather flutter, they knew the person was not breathing. Other tests included shining a bright light into the patient's eyes and using a pin to prick the skin.

No reaction meant death was fairly certain. When the body lost its natural color and felt cold, those in attendance knew for sure that the person was no longer alive.

Today we have more scientific means of determining death. Doctors monitor all life processes to be sure there is no hope of recovery. But advances in medical science have not provided a simple answer to the question, What is death? And when, exactly, does it occur? The fact is that death does not occur all at once. It is a process—it happens over a period of time. A person normally starts to die when the heartbeat and respiration stop. This means that the blood, which carries oxygen, is no longer circulating to all parts of the body. Without oxygen the brain begins to die. Some brain cells die in three to six minutes. Psychiatrist and physician Michael A. Simpson says, "Once the brain cells die they will never regain their function." He explains that other body cells are tougher, and it takes longer for them to die. For instance, muscle cells may react to electrical impulses (shocks) for two hours after all other organs have stopped functioning. Hair and fingernails may continue to grow for a day or more.

Technology changes the definition

Today a heart that has stopped beating momentarily can be started again. This organ can then be kept alive. The person may recover and live a normal life. Thus the loss of a heartbeat is not a sure sign of death.

In some circumstances, a brain that has stopped working can start up again on its own. This can happen after a person has taken drugs called barbiturates, or has suffered extreme cold. But if enough brain cells have been damaged, there is a point at which the personality is gone. Dr. Simpson explains, "You can lose all the brain with which you think, love, quarrel, and otherwise consciously exist, but continue breathing as a 'vegetable.'" Is this life or is it death? This is a question doctors—and all of us—must try to answer.

A healthy, normal brain generates millions of tiny electrical charges,

Wizard of Id / By Brant Parker and Johnny Hart

called brain waves. These waves can be measured and recorded. To do this, doctors use a machine called an electroencephalograph (EEG). Wires from the EEG are attached to the person's head (this is painless). If the machine records no brain activity for twenty-four hours the person is considered brain-dead. Brain-death specialists check to make sure the person is not suffering from hypothermia (exposure to intense cold). They also check to make sure the person has no barbiturates in his or her system. Then the specialists do two separate EEG tests before pronouncing the person legally dead.

Legal definitions

In 1981, the President's Commission for the Study of Ethical Problems in Medicine and Biomedical and Behavioral Research recommended that a law be adopted throughout the United States. This law sets the rules for deciding when a person is legally dead. It is paraphrased as follows:

Uniform Determination of Death Act
A person whose blood no longer circulates through his or her system is dead if specialists cannot start the blood circulating again. A person who has stopped breathing is dead if specialists cannot start respiration again. A person whose entire brain has stopped functioning is dead if specialists cannot start brain function again.

Arkansas bases its definition of death on the above guidelines. However, this state expresses it more simply:

> A person is legally dead when the brain has . . . ceased to function and there is an absence of . . . breath.

By 1989, forty-four states had brain-death laws. Twenty-nine of these laws are based on the Commission's recommendations. Daniel Wikler, Ph.D., of the University of Wisconsin Medical School, says the diagnosis of brain death "is as certain as anything in medicine. . . . Clinicians can tell which patients have permanent loss of all brain function."

Need for timely transplants

The question of when death actually occurs is an important one. For instance, if a man dies an hour before his life insurance goes into effect his widow will receive no insurance money.

But another concern has arisen in recent years. We live in an age when organs from one person can be transplanted into the body of another. A kidney may be transplanted from one living person to another. But a heart can only be transplanted after the donor is legally dead.

If a transplant is to work, the tissue must be alive and healthy. If an organ's cells have begun to die, that organ cannot be used by another human being. A heart is usable for only six to eight hours after brain death.

When to take an organ for transplantation is a question that is usually decided by the doctors, clergy, and the family together. For the husband, wife, or child of the newly brain-dead patient still breathing artificially on a respirator, it is difficult to accept the fact that death has occurred. Yet, if the transplant is to be successful, they must decide fairly quickly.

Death, when it comes, is final. Sometimes it is called "the final mystery." It is, however, a mystery that most people do not really want to solve. Humans work at preventing death all their lives.

Efforts to prevent death begin as soon as a baby is born. A newborn is wrapped in blankets or placed in a warm environment so it will not die of exposure to the cold. When it is older the parents worry that their child may not be eating the right foods to keep it strong and healthy. "Eat your breakfast, Sally," a father says. "We don't want you to starve to death!" Later this father may say, "Get down off that ladder—you'll fall and break your neck!"

Said half in jest, warnings such as these nevertheless serve to make a child aware of how precious life is. They also make the child aware of how carefully life must be nurtured and guarded.

Warnings continue into the teen years and adulthood. "Drive carefully," a mother tells her son. And a billboard along his route reinforces her advice.

Automobile accidents

Despite our efforts, we all die sometime. One of the most common causes of death in our society is automobile accidents. People of all ages are at risk of dying in accidents involving motor vehicles, but among young people these accidents are the leading cause of fatalities.

Heidi, a high school sophomore, lost her best friend when Betsy was hit by a car. Betsy was walking along a road near her suburban home after a football game. It was dark, and Betsy was wearing a maroon letter jacket and black jeans. A car came from behind and struck Betsy. She died before an ambulance could get her to the hospital.

Betsy's death shocked the students in her school. Advice they had heard all their lives about wearing something light-colored when walking at night, having reflective trim on their clothes, and staying to the left side of the road took on new meaning.

There was also a question as to whether the driver who hit Betsy had been drinking. Jenny, a teenager quoted in the *Minneapolis Star*

Police and fire officials inspect the mangled remains of two cars involved in a fatal collision in Lexington, Massachusetts. Automobile accidents are a common cause of death in the U.S.

Tribune told about the feelings that accompany a death caused by a drunk driver:

> My father was killed by a drunk driver. You can't really describe what that feels like. . . . It's definitely worse than if it had been a heart attack or something like that, because there's this overwhelming sense that it shouldn't have happened. . . . He didn't die—somebody killed him.

Jenny thinks that stiffer laws dealing with drunk drivers may help prevent such deaths. Many legislators agree, and laws with stiffer penalties are being put in force.

Every year more than twenty-five thousand people are killed in alcohol-related crashes. Tranquilizers, marijuana, and a variety of other drugs also affect the mental and physical skills needed for safe driving.

Motor vehicle deaths are of great concern, especially for young people. But for society as a whole, illness is the leading cause of death.

Fighting off disease

Even in earliest times people tried to cure the sick to prevent death. In his book *The Final Mystery*, Stanley Klein says that early people "thought of illness as a punishment, perhaps sent by some angry god. Or they believed that an evil spirit coming to live inside the body was the cause of pain or sickness." So early attempts at preventing death centered around making peace with the angry god, or making the evil spirits go away. Prayers, magic, and medicines combined to form ancient cures. Sometimes the success of the "medicine men" who performed these cures was just lucky chance. Still, reports Klein, "Five-thousand-year-old medical books used in Egypt have been found. And ancient Indian doctors knew a great deal about curative drugs made from plants, and were in some cases able to perform operations."

The practice of medicine changed from magic to a science in ancient Greece. Hippocrates, born in Greece in 460 B.C., is credited with the idea that every illness has a natural cause. He also said that a person's way of life—the food she eats, the work she does, the climate she lives in—can contribute to either sickness or health. Doctors and scientists have taken Hippocrates' ideas and expanded on them. Today, they have more knowledge of nutrition, stress, and sanitation, plus vaccines and modern methods of medical care. Because of this knowledge, specialists can often prevent fatal diseases such as cholera, tuberculosis, and smallpox. But other diseases still plague us.

Heart disease claims more lives than any other illness in the United States. Heart attacks are the most common form of this killer. A heart attack occurs when part of the heart muscle is damaged and is unable to pump enough blood to keep a person alive. Not all heart attacks are fatal, however. The American Heart Association explains that

if the heart can be kept beating, and not too much heart muscle is damaged, small blood vessels may gradually reroute blood

Fifteen Leading Causes of Death in the United States

Rank	Cause of death	Rate	Percent of total deaths
. . .	All causes	873.9	100.0
1	Diseases of heart	323.0	37.0
2	Malignant neoplasms, including neoplasms of lymphatic and hematopoietic tissues (cancers)	193.3	22.1
3	Cerebrovascular disease (strokes)	64.1	7.3
4	Accidents and adverse effects	19.2	. . .
. . .	Motor vehicle accidents	19.2	. . .
. . .	All other accidents and adverse effects	19.9	. . .
5	Chronic obstructive pulmonary diseases and allied conditions	31.3	3.6
6	Pneumonia and influenza	28.3	3.2
7	Diabetes melitus	15.5	1.8
8	Suicide	12.3	1.4
9	Chronic liver disease and cirhosis	11.2	1.3
10	Atherosclerosis	10.0	1.1
11	Nephritis, nephrotic syndrome, and nephrosis	8.9	1.0
12	Homicide and legal intervention	8.3	1.0
13	Certain conditions originating in the perinatal period	8.1	0.9
14	Septicemia	7.2	0.8
15	Congenital anomalies	5.4	0.6
. . .	All other causes	107.8	12.3

SOURCE: Ninth Revision, International Classification of Diseases, 1975.

around the blocked arteries. This is the heart's own way of compensating for the clogged artery. . . . In many cases, if trained medical professionals are immediately available, they can get the heart beating again by using electrical shock and/or drugs. . . . The key to surviving a heart attack is promptly recognizing the warning signals and getting immediate medical attention.

Cancer is the second greatest killer. A cancer is a malignant growth in a person's body. Cancers tend to spread, but in some cases surgery will stop the spreading. When the cancer involves blood-forming tissues and causes an abnormal increase in bone marrow, it is called leukemia. Transplants and drugs can sometimes cure leukemia. New methods of cancer treatment are constantly being developed, and doctors are hopeful that when they determine why cancer starts, they will find a cure.

Preventing strokes

Strokes are the third largest cause of death. A stroke occurs when the flow of blood to the brain is blocked. Strokes also occur when a diseased artery in the brain bursts, flooding the surrounding tissue with blood. This is called a cerebral hemorrhage. Hemorrhage of an artery in the brain may also be caused by a head injury.

Doctors cannot fix the damage to the brain after a stroke. So preventing a stroke is very important. The American Heart Association lists the following ways to lower the chances of having either a heart attack or stroke:

Have your blood pressure checked once a year.
Do not smoke cigarettes.
Eat nutritious food in moderate amounts.
Have regular medical checkups.

Part or all of the brain may be damaged in a stroke. However, in some situations the person may recover and go on to live a long time with only slight impairment to some functions.

After these top three causes of death come other diseases such as diabetes mellitus, liver disease, pneumonia, and influenza. Medical professionals are working constantly to conquer all known diseases. However, when little is known about a disease, many deaths occur before methods of prevention or a cure can be found. AIDS, a fairly new disease, is such a case.

Acquired Immunodeficiency Syndrome, or AIDS, was brought to the attention of the public in 1981. At that time physcans and public health officials began to notice an unusual number of strange infections in homosexual men and people who injected themselves with drugs. Hemophiliacs, who suffer from a blood disease and must have frequent transfusions, also have been affected. Today, AIDS is spreading through the general population as well. When a person has AIDS, his or her immune system does not function properly. Therefore, the person cannot fight off disease. Researchers have determined that AIDS is caused by a virus and so far is always fatal. This virus can be transmitted from one person to another through body fluids such as blood and semen.

At this time, there is no known cure for AIDS. Thus prevention is vitally important. Health care workers, such as surgeons, dentists, and others, wear protective gloves. People who have sexual intercourse can reduce their risk by using condoms. Drug users are urged to use only sterile needles and to not share them with friends.

"AIDS is a life-threatening disease and a major public health issue," said C. Everett Koop, M.D., in the Surgeon General's Report on AIDS. "Its impact on our society is and will continue to be devastating."

Alzheimer's disease

Alzheimer's disease is not new, but because it affects older people, and because more people are living longer, it is of increasing concern.

Imagine having a grandmother who does not know who you are

today even though she knew you yesterday. Or imagine a grandfather who goes shopping at his favorite grocery store and then cannot find his way home. These are the kinds of things that happen to victims of Alzheimer's disease. Most of these people are over sixty-five years old. They have trouble remembering things and are easily confused. They may be quarrelsome where they were formerly easygoing.

When a person has Alzheimer's, his or her memory goes first, then the body slowly fails. Since this is a degenerative disease, it continues to worsen over a period of from six to eight years. Some people with Alzheimer's linger on for as long as twenty years.

There is no cure for Alzheimer's, but scientists are hopeful that as they learn more about this disease, help will be found for its victims.

A Boston woman attempting suicide is rescued by emergency workers. Severe depression is the most common reason people attempt suicide. Thirty thousand Americans succeed in taking their lives each year.

Diseases and accidents are the leading causes of death for all ages. However, two other categories are among the first fifteen causes listed by the U.S. National Center for Health Statistics in a 1987 report. These are suicide and homicide (murder). Suicide ranked eighth in the list of causes; homicide ranked twelfth.

Death by suicide

Most people spend a good deal of their lives trying to avoid death, yet some people choose to die.

Every year in the United States, thirty thousand people die by their own hand. White males over age thirty-five are the most frequent victims. Of these, men between the ages of seventy and seventy-five are at the greatest risk. But in 1987, approximately six thousand people under the age of twenty-five took their own lives. Three hundred of these were under fifteen years old—twice as many as in 1980. Though suicide is shocking at any age, it is especially tragic when it involves a young person.

Why would anyone choose to die? Those who study suicides have learned that most people who take their own lives are severely depressed. This means they are so unhappy that they find no hope, no joy, in living. Unlike the "down" feelings that all of us experience from time to time, a person who is clinically depressed (needs to be treated medically) has been feeling this way for a long time. Author Judie Smith, in her book *Coping with Suicide*, says a deep depression "is not like an illness for which researchers can isolate a germ in a test tube or develop a vaccine." But when properly diagnosed it can be treated with medication and counseling.

Though most suicides kill themselves because they find their lives too painful, the act may serve other purposes. One teenager who considered suicide was angry with her parents for the rules they imposed on her behavior. "They'll be sorry when I'm gone," she told a counselor. The girl failed to realize that she would not be around to enjoy her revenge if she carried out her threat. Counselors worry that some young people do not understand how final death is.

Suicide can also be used as a means of escaping blame and guilt for something bad someone has done. "One of the most common triggers of suicide in children and teens is a humiliating experience, like getting caught stealing," says Ann Epstein, a child psychiatrist at Harvard Medical School.

An athlete who will be confined to a wheelchair for the rest of her life because of an accident said, "I'd be better off dead." Everyone says things like this at one time or another, but most of us finds ways to cope with our problems.

Occasionally, a person who has had a dramatic change in his life may feel that he cannot cope. A classic example of this is the businesspeople in the late 1920s and early 1930s who lost tremendous wealth when the stock market crashed. They could not face the state of poverty they had been plunged into, and chose instead to end their lives.

Clustered suicides

A puzzling—and frightening—aspect of suicide in recent years is "clustering." Clustering means that several suicides happen in a short period of time. Is suicide contagious? Or are these people copying the behavior of someone else? Psychiatrists believe that suicides do not happen "out of the blue." A person who commits the act has given it much thought. The decision to do it may be triggered by learning that someone else has just done it. Perhaps this makes it seem all right.

Finally, an attempt at suicide is often the ultimate cry for help. For instance, the victim wants help but is unable to ask for it. She pops a handful of pills into her mouth just before her family is due home from work. She expects to be found and rushed to the hospital before the pills can take effect. If she is found in time, she may get the help she needs. If the family is delayed, another tragedy occurs.

Two-thirds of would-be suicides relay serious signals of distress by their words or behavior. Sometimes statements like "I might be going away for awhile" should not be ignored. A simple question, Why?, may open up a conversation that will prevent a death. A common misconception is that people who talk about suicide do not do it. This is not true. Talking about suicide is a chief danger sign. Most people who commit suicide have told someone about their idea. They may not be just looking for attention. A friend should listen and look for other signs of distress. These include:

A long-standing depression
Changes in eating and sleeping patterns
A slip in school grades
Disinterest in appearance and neglect of physical hygiene
Changes in personality (moodiness, acting "wild," or
    always being tired)
Gaining or losing weight
Taking up a dangerous sport, such as skydiving
Taking other unnecessary risks
Giving away favorite possessions such as a camera
    or a bicycle
Increasing use of drugs and alcohol

If warning signs are present, author Judie Smith says, it is time to offer assistance. "Don't tell a person he is silly to be thinking about suicide. Accept his feelings and refer him to a school counselor, a telephone hot line, or a crisis intervention center."

Suicide prevention centers

Approximately 175 to 200 suicide prevention centers are located throughout the United States. Metro-Help, Inc., located in Chicago, operates a toll-free, twenty-four-hour suicide hotline. Help is available in all fifty states through this organization. Its number is 1-800-621-4000.

Calvin and Hobbes / By Bill Watterson

Feelings of despair may be only temporary. Knowing this, a reader of Ann Landers's advice column had these words for anyone considering ending his or her life: "Suicide is a permanent solution to a temporary problem. Those who love you want you around, problems and all."

Up until the last decades suicide was considered a crime in many states. But people who attempted it were rarely brought to trial. Author Smith says, "Even though suicide is no longer illegal, there is still confusion [about the legality] in some people's minds. It is perfectly clear, however, that the law does not permit aiding in someone else's suicide." Thus a woman who bought poison for a friend, knowing how he was going to use it, is guilty of a serious crime.

Violent death

Over 25,000 Americans die in homicides (murders) each year. Joanne E. Bernstein, in her book *Loss*, describes one such incident:

> Myron's father ran a cleaning store. One summer evening, when Myron was twelve, his dad descended the stairs from their apartment above the store, ready to resume business after dinner. "Go down and help Daddy," urged Myron's mother, as her son dawdled over dessert. Five minutes later a shot was heard. Myron's father was killed.

Bernstein comments that, "Murder, like a senseless accident, seems such a waste." Presumably Myron's father was killed by someone who was about to rob his store. This is sometimes the motivation for murder. Other homicides come about because of carelessness, anger, jealousy, or other violent emotions.

In the United States, we call these careless or emotion-based killings manslaughter. They are regarded as less serious than a murder that is committed "in cold blood"—that is, planned and deliberately carried out. However, the result is the same—someone is dead, and others are left to handle the feelings of grief and anger that come when a person is murdered.

There are laws against murder and punishments for committing it. But it is difficult to determine whether they help prevent homicide.

Two other frequent causes of death are listed by the National Center for Health Statistics. They are natural disasters and war.

A lone visitor walks through the morning mist at Arlington National Cemetery near Washington, D.C. Thousands of white crosses mark the graves of soldiers who died in America's wars.

When tornadoes, hurricanes, and floods are expected, warnings go out. Lives are saved as people seek shelter or flee to higher ground. But in the case of earthquakes and in areas where communication is poor, little can be done to prevent such deaths.

Wars take a heavy toll of military personnel and innocent victims alike. Buff Bradley, in his book *Endings*, says, "It is possible to say that human history is the history of war—one war after another for thousands of years." It is not likely that war will be prevented in the near future. Until human nature changes, war will be another way that lives are ended.

How Long Can You Expect to Live?

ATTAINED AGE	MALE	FEMALE	AVERAGE
0	70.3	77.9	74.1
1	71.2	78.7	75.0
10	71.5	78.9	75.3
20	72.0	79.2	75.6
30	72.9	79.5	76.3
40	73.8	80.0	76.9
50	75.1	80.9	78.1
60	77.6	82.5	80.2
70	81.5	85.1	83.5
80	86.9	89.0	88.2
85 and Up	90.2	91.7	91.2

SOURCE: National Center for Health Statistics
U.S. Department of Health and Human Services (1981)

What are the chances of escaping fatal diseases, accidents, suicide, murder, natural disasters, and war? People living in the United States can expect to live to be 70 years old or more. The older they get, the greater their life expectancy. For instance, a person who is now 15 years old may expect to live to be 75.4 years old. If he lives to be 70, he can expect to be alive at 83.5 years.

According to the *Guiness Book of World Records*, the oldest woman living in 1988 was 112 years old. The oldest man was 111.

John Evans, the man who lived to be 111 years old, was interviewed by a newspaper reporter. Evans credited his long life to "eating honey every day, and never smoking, drinking, or swearing." He said singing also helps!

Dr. Lawrence Lamb, who writes an advice column for the News America Syndicate, had more scientific advice for those concerned with life span:

> You can do a lot to increase your chances of living your potential life span. As an example, the leading cause of cancer deaths in both men and women is lung cancer, and more than 80 percent of these deaths would not occur if people did not smoke. You can also follow recommendations to decrease your risk of heart attacks and strokes. That includes your diet and exercise.
>
> The feeble state of many older people is a result of disuse that has allowed the body to become feeble. Much of this can be prevented by a proper physical fitness program that is a regular and continuing effort. You can also exercise your mind to help keep it in shape.

Dr. Lamb says that new information has led scientists to believe that if everything were "just right" we could expect to live to be 115 years old!

CHAPTER TWO

When Someone Is Dying

A death that comes suddenly has to be dealt with only by the survivors. There is nothing that can be done for the dead. But when a person dies slowly from a terminal illness, the patient has a long time to think about what lies ahead. This period can be a painful time, full of loneliness and fear. But it can also be a period when a person has the opportunity to reflect on the meaning of life, to say goodbye to loved ones, and to take care of unfinished business. The latter may be practical things such as writing a will. Or it may be making peace with someone with whom the dying person has had a poor relationship in the past.

Most people who are dying are aware of their condition. They have seen TV shows about people with cancer. They have known others who have died of heart attacks. They may have given to fund drives for diseases that are common killers. When they are diagnosed as having one of these life-shortening illnesses, their impending death is no surprise. Dr. Elisabeth Kübler-Ross has led and participated in over seven hundred workshops, lectures, and seminars on the care of dying patients. She does not believe that patients should be told that they are dying until they ask. In her book *Questions and Answers on Death and Dying*, Kübler-Ross says:

I do not encourage people to force patients to face their own death when they are not ready for it. Patients should be told that they are seriously ill. When they are ready to bring up the issue of death and dying, we should answer them, we should listen to them, and we should hear the questions, but you do not go around telling patients they are dying and depriving them of a glimpse of hope that they may need in order to live until they die.

This authority on death and dying also believes it is cruel and unnecessary to pretend that a person will surely get well. To do so is like playing an unfair game. She says that in talking to a dying person it is better to be "honest about your feelings of fear, loss, and separation." In this way family and friends can express what is called anticipatory grief. This is a sadness that comes when we know that death is not far away. Feelings of anticipatory grief help prepare the survivors for death when it finally comes.

It is not easy to talk about dying, and it is not only friends and family who find this to be true. Health professionals, too, find the topic difficult to deal with. Death is, in a way, an embarrassment. Science has failed to find ways to keep it from happening. Doctors who have vowed to cure the sick may look at death as an enemy.

Until a branch of science called thanatology (the study of death) gained status, it seemed improper to ask questions of those who were terminally ill. But Dr. Kübler-Ross interviewed and counseled hundreds of terminally ill patients. Many of them wanted to talk about their feelings. From these interviews, Dr. Kübler-Ross developed a pattern. In her book *On Death and Dying*, she lists five stages the dying go through.

Shock and denial

When they first become aware that their illness is terminal, most people react with disbelief. They may say "No! Not me. It can't be true." This is typical whether they were told outright of their

Sally Forth / By Greg Howard

coming death or have realized it on their own.

In this stage they are sure their X rays have been mixed up with those of another patient. They are convinced that the laboratory is wrong, or that there must be *some* mistake somewhere.

Denial is used by almost all patients, not only in the first stages, but from time to time later on. It is too difficult to face death all the time. The patient must put the possibility of her own death away for a while to pursue life. This does not mean that she will not be willing or even happy and relieved to talk about her impending death at a later date. But such discussion must be postponed until the patient is ready to face it. Very few patients deny death to the very end. Dr. Kübler-Ross says that most patients gradually stop denying that they are dying.

Anger

When it finally becomes clear to the patient that she is really dying, she will no longer say it cannot be true, but will ask, WHY ME? Denial has been replaced by feelings of anger, rage, envy, and resentment. These may be directed at the doctor and nurses, family members, or anyone who is available. It is a difficult time for everyone. Who would not be angry? All this person's life activities are being interrupted. She will not be able to finish the cabin she is building, take the trip she planned, or watch the children graduate from high school. Of course the dying patient resents everyone who can still enjoy these things.

If visitors and staff realize that this anger has little to do with the people who become its target, they can take it less personally. In time, Kübler-Ross says, a patient who is respected, understood, and given the necessary attention will let much of this anger go.

Bargaining

In the third stage, the patient wants to bargain. She may bargain with God for an extension of life, or promise good behavior and religious dedication if she is spared more suffering. An example of this is the woman who pleaded, "If you'll just let me live to see my daughter married, then I'll be a good patient." According to Kübler-Ross, this woman told the doctors and nurses, "If God grants me this, I'll do everything you ask." But, Kübler-Ross adds, "None of our patients have 'kept their promises.'" The woman got her wish,

Dr. Elisabeth Kübler-Ross, shown here at her Virginia home, was a pioneer in the scientific study of death and dying.

returned to the hospital, and was as cantankerous as ever. "Now don't forget, I have a second daughter," she reminded the nurses.

When the terminally ill patient can no longer fight her illness and her knowledge of death, she is filled with a great sense of loss. She is likely to slip into the fourth stage of dying.

Depression

In this stage the patient realizes she is about to lose everything and everyone she ever loved. The sadness is overwhelming. An understanding person is needed to listen to her concerns. Words of encouragement and efforts to cheer up the patient are ineffective. The patient is now preparing for death, and grieving in anticipation. "If she is allowed to express her sorrow she will find a final acceptance much easier, and she will be grateful to those who can sit with her during this stage of depression without constantly telling her not to be sad," says Kübler-Ross.

When unfinished business has been settled, the patient becomes quiet. There is no longer a need for words. Kübler-Ross says the supportive friend or relative will try to do what the patient wants. Understanding can be expressed with a touch of a hand or just silently sitting together. If the patient indicates he no longer wants visitors, it should not be taken personally. He is preparing himself emotionally for what lies ahead.

Acceptance

In the fifth, and final, stage—acceptance—patients are neither depressed nor angry. They are no longer struggling against death, but are almost without feelings. It is as if the pain of parting with life is gone and they have found some peace. While these patients may still feel sad about losing life, they may welcome knowing that the end is near, especially if there has been great physical pain.

Kübler-Ross stresses that not everyone reaches the final stage of acceptance. Nor do they follow all stages in order, but may go back and forth between stages. Other thanatologists agree. One of these, Dr. Stephen Gullo, says people die in the manner that is most comfortable for them. He places dying patients in six categories.

Dr. Gullo's categories

Some people, according to Dr. Gullo, are Death Deniers. They accept the fact that they are seriously ill but refuse to believe they will die.

Death Acceptors look at their chances realistically and, when all resources have been exhausted, they accept the inevitable and grieve for their losses.

Death Submitters give in, often refusing to take medicine or to believe there is any hope of getting well. They feel doomed and are passive victims of illness.

Death Facilitators refuse all help and may actively try to hasten their own death. They may commit suicide. They do not want to die, but they cannot go on living with a terminal illness.

Death Transcenders take another approach. These people accept death as a part of a larger outlook on life. They believe death is a final stage of life, one which comes before an afterlife. To them, death is intertwined with their religion.

Dr. Gullo calls people in the last category the Death Defiers. These people are engaged in a ceaseless battle with fate. They will hang on as long as possible, enjoying whatever they can, and maintaining their independence right up to the end.

Individuals face death differently

Dying people are individuals. They use the time they have left in whatever way they see fit. One man chose not only what music he wanted played at his memorial service, but what kind of flowers he wanted placed on his casket. He even went so far as to specify the kind of sandwiches he wanted served after his funeral. A dying

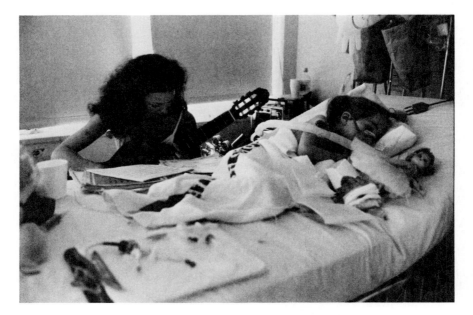

The mother of a critically ill child softly plays a guitar in her daughter's hospital room. Many people believe that creating a warm, positive atmosphere around a sick person aids the recovery process. For the dying, it eases the physical and emotional distress of death.

woman gave a party in her hospital room and ordered champagne and cake for her family and friends. These acts show a healthy acceptance of death, and these people are taking care of unfinished business.

Norman Cousins chose to spend his time in a way that resulted in his recovery. Hospitalized in 1964 with a life-threatening disease, he developed his own medication—laughter. He watched old Marx Brothers movies and other reruns of films that made him laugh. Cousins is now attempting to find a scientific basis to support the age-old theory that "laughter is the best medicine."

There is no doubt that attitude plays an important part in coping with disease—and with dying. Each person will develop his or her own style.

Near-death experiences

But what about the very moment of death itself? The time when life is gone from the body, never to return? Will it hurt? What will it be like?

Some people think they know.

Kevin Vida was fifteen years old when he climbed high up into a tree in his backyard to check out the view. According to an article in *McCall's* magazine,

> On his way down, a nearby power line brushed the tree, shooting 27,000 volts of electricity through his body and locking his joints so tightly he couldn't release the branch. . . . "For a second, everything turned blue," Kevin recalls, "and all I could think of was, What am I going to tell Mom—that I just got electrocuted in a tree?"

Kevin's brother found him dangling in the tree and managed to pry him loose. Luckily the older boy knew how to administer CPR (cardiopulmonary resuscitation), and in four minutes Kevin's heart started beating again. Meanwhile, Kevin had what scientists call a near-death experience (NDE). This is how Kevin remembers it:

> After I passed out, I found myself walking along a path in a humongous forest. I'd never seen anything like it, but I knew for sure I wasn't dreaming. This was *real*. At first I was afraid, but then I saw my grandfather, who had died about a year earlier. He kept reassuring me, "Keep going, you'll be fine."
>
> I began to sense something warm above me, so I looked up and saw an incredible light—crystal-clear and brighter than the sun, but you could look right into it without hurting your eyes. Inside the light was the figure of a man with his hand held out to me, radiating so much love. . . . It was the most beautiful feeling I've ever experienced. I never wanted to leave.

Kevin was in the hospital for two weeks. After several months' recuperation, he was able to resume most of his normal activities. But he says, "For a long time I was angry. I didn't understand why I had to come back. I wished God had just taken me. But now I think he put me here for a reason, to help other people. That's what matters most."

Kevin is doing just that by working as an emergency medical technician by day and volunteering on an ambulance squad at night.

Effect of an NDE

"After [an NDE] the person can never again return to the former way of being," writes Kenneth Ring, Ph.D., a professor of psychology. It changes one's life. Researcher Bruce Greyson, M.C., points out that "suicide attempters who've had NDEs come back to the same problems they had before, but they now see these problems as challenges and opportunities for growth."

According to a Gallup poll, eight to nine million Americans have reported similar sensations while "temporarily dead" or on the verge of death. They describe feeling peaceful and loved. Some heard beautiful music; many had the sense of being on a journey, often traveling to a light just beyond a border or a gate. To religious persons this border was interpreted as the gates of heaven. But even for atheists, the experience was essentially the same.

In some instances the person sees his or her whole life pass in review, as in the expression, "My life passed before my eyes." One woman said she relived events from her childhood, smelling every smell and feeling every emotion. She suddenly realized how much her parents had loved her. Her "whole life started to make sense."

Some people have described what is called an out-of-body episode. A man who had a heart attack said, "I knew I was dead. But the nurses and doctors kept working over me. I floated out of my own physical body, away from the loud, echoing, buzzing noises, and

Nineteenth-century French artist Gustave Doré's woodcut depicts the entrance to heaven. Doré's woodcut looks remarkably like the "tunnel" described by people who have had near-death experiences.

moved rapidly down a long passage.'' Later he felt himself go back into his own body.

Are these experiences real? Many scientists believe they may be, but some are skeptical. They maintain that drugs might produce similar effects. This does not, however, explain what Kevin Vida experienced when he was not on drugs.

Not all NDEs are pleasant

It is comforting to think that death may be a pleasant experience, but it may not be so for everyone. About 1 to 2 percent of the NDEs reported in the Gallup poll were unpleasant experiences. Some of this type were also reported in a 1962 study of patients suffering from heart attacks. These were "intense and disturbing" fantasies. They included violence such as being killed in an automobile crash, shooting one's way out of the hospital only to be killed by an evil nurse, and falling out of a wheelchair and being run over by it.

Kevin Vida's NDE has both disturbing and comforting aspects to it. When his doctors asked him why he was at first afraid, Kevin said that while he was in the forest he was grabbed by a horrible-looking man with scars and serpents crawling on him. It was his grandfather's encouragement that kept him going.

Accounts of near-death experiences are not new. In 1892, Albert Heim, a Swiss geologist and mountain climber, wrote about interviews he had with thirty people who survived falls from the rugged walls of the Alps. Many of them reported that in just a few seconds they had hundreds of memories and "visions" of their lives. They also felt shock, fear, and disbelief that this could be happening to them. Then came anger—I don't want to die! It isn't fair! they said to themselves. Some said they experienced feelings of calmness just before they lost consciousness. These thoughts and feelings were much like those of people in more recent studies. They are also remarkably like the five stages of death that Kübler-Ross defines.

A few researchers worry that the popular portrayal of blissful NDEs might encourage depressed people to commit suicide in the belief that death will be wonderful. Others say it is important to remember that death may not always be calm and pleasant.

Author Buff Bradley has some comforting thoughts in his book *Endings*:

> From all the studies that have been done, we can gather that whether you die fast or slowly, your mind seems to have a certain ability to adjust, to calm itself, to prepare itself for the end and maybe even make death a peaceful, sometimes joyful experience. All of us wonder, from time to time, how we'll do at dying. Maybe we can take some comfort from knowing that even in the face of death, the human mind has a way of taking pretty good care of itself.

Caring for the dying

When a family learns that one of its members is terminally ill, they often go through the same feelings of denial, anger, bargaining, depression, and acceptance that the patient does. They may not experience all stages, and not in any particular order. However, what they feel, and how they deal with these feelings, influences the care that the patient receives.

Dr. Kübler-Ross says, "Most patients prefer to die at home, but there are a few who prefer to die in a hospital. Mothers, for example, who do not want to expose their children to the final crisis, or people who have been very lonely and have had poor family relationships, sometimes prefer to die in an institution."

Cared for at home, the dying person has the comfort of being in a familiar environment with possessions, pets, family, and friends close by. Children can share in the patient's last days, bringing a glass of water or watching TV with the person. Kübler-Ross describes a case where a young girl was dying. Her bed was placed in the living room where she could watch for her little brother to come home from school each day. They spent precious hours sharing his adventures.

The mother was there to give comfort at all hours, and for them, this was the best way to deal with the child's death.

For others, the presence of a dying person in the house may cause so much stress that it is not a desirable choice. For instance, with a bed in the living room, other family members cannot entertain visitors. Also, the dying person may not have the privacy he or she prefers. Even when someone gives up a bedroom for the patient, conflicts may arise. Routines are upset, and family members may find it difficult to cope with illness every hour of the day. Often a combination of hospital care and frequent home visits is possible.

Hospitals, with their modern methods of treatment, may be able to keep a patient alive longer than if the patient were at home. This may or may not be the best course of action. Judith Paterson, in an article in the *Minneapolis Star Tribune*, told how she felt about her seventy-eight-year-old stepmother being in intensive care for long periods of time:

> There I see hopeless cases kept alive for no reason. Cancer patients without hope of recovery get chemotherapy, blood transfusions, radiation. The very old lie like corpses in their beds, liquids dripping all day into limbs crisp and yellow as parchment. A social worker calls it the "ritual of prolongation." I ask "what for?" and get no answer.

Medical personnel are beginning to realize that when death is near, it may be kinder to make dying easier than to keep the patient alive. Because of this, the hospice system has been incorporated into hospital care.

Hospice

Hospices began in England. They were separate buildings, meant to be a combination of home and hospital. The emphasis was on comfort for the terminally ill patient, in an atmosphere where the family could visit in pleasant surroundings.

In America, hospice care has come to mean a special kind of care

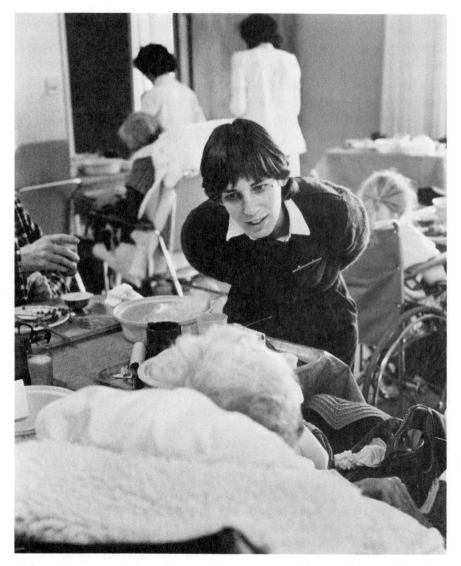

A hospice nurse visits with a patient at a convalescent home. Hospices provide care and services specifically for the dying. Whether caring for the dying person at home or in a special facility, hospice-style care can help people die peacefully and with dignity.

for the dying patient within the hospital or at home. Patients and their families know they are dying, so there is no pretense. Medical care is given as needed. Pain-killing drugs are given more readily than in regular hospital situations where addiction is feared. In hospice care the next dose comes before the last one has worn off, so dying can be free of pain. If a patient chooses not to take drugs in order to avoid the drowsiness that may accompany them, that choice is honored. Some people would rather endure some pain to stay alert and clear-headed as they experience their last days of life. Hospice care encourages patients to live as fully as possible until the time of death. It strives, too, to meet the needs of the family.

An American Cancer Society publication says, "At the root of the philosophy of hospice is the belief that death does not represent failure, but is rather a natural, and ideally, triumphant rite of passage."

Problems with hospice care

The Society does point out some potential problems that are of concern to health professionals. One is continuity of care. The patient in a hospice may become separate from the physicians who have provided care through the earlier phases of illness, causing the patient to feel abandoned. Also, in some hospices, services such as those that can be provided by a well-organized hospital laboratory are inadequate.

Some of the major hospices are interested in research, but many are not: their emphasis is clearly on day-to-day patient care. The American Cancer Society is in favor of research, commenting,

> If we remain dependent on our current approaches, we will continue to see thousands of cancer patients who, despite our best efforts, suffer for a considerable period of time before their death. The problems of the dying cancer patient are legitimate subjects for research.
>
> Regardless of their state of disease, patients may wish to maintain hope for a lengthy survival. The opportunity for hospice patients to participate in research may not only keep open the

door of hope but also contribute to their need to maintain a sense of dignity. We all search for meaning in our lives, and participation in a research program provides a chance for a direct contribution to the fight against cancer. The patient's sense of dignity is enhanced if he is able to maintain a participatory rather than a purely passive role.

The same may be said of patients with any type of terminal illness. A patient who is somehow involved in her own care often feels better than the patient who has nothing to do but lie in bed.

Emotional needs as important as physical

It is clear that those concerned with the welfare of the dying must take care of the patient's physical needs. But the patient's social, emotional, and spiritual needs require attention as well. Family and friends can help.

It may be hard to spend time with a dying person. But visiting that person, talking over good times in the past, even crying together at the sadness of parting, are ways for both the patient and the survivors to say goodbye. Buff Bradley tells how he spent time with a terminally ill friend:

> Patrick was in the hospital nearly every day for the last year of his life. I used to take my lunch there and we'd eat on the lawn sometimes, or at other times in his room if he was hooked up for transfusions or intravenous feedings. When he could get out for a few hours, which he loved to do, we'd go for pizza or to see a film.
>
> Patrick died in 1974, just before his fourteenth birthday.

Bradley says, "I still do not understand his suffering. I still do not know all of the things I felt, and feel, about it." But Bradley spent quality time with someone who was dying. He realizes this is not an easy thing to do. But he reminds us that dying people are the same people they were before, only now they are dealing with life's last serious business. They need comfort and companionship.

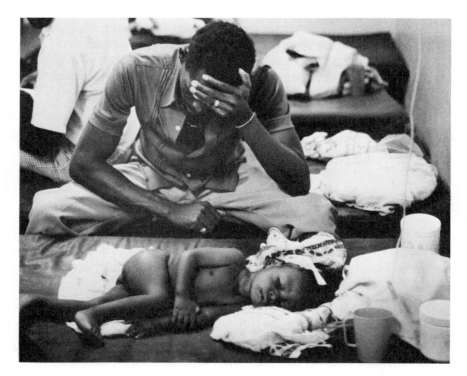

An anxious father keeps vigil over his seriously ill child. When someone we know and love is near death it is normal to experience strong, and often painful, emotions of grief, anxiety, fear, and even anger.

Talk can center around the things both parties have always been interested in—TV shows, family projects, sports. But a new topic may be introduced: death. Dying people often want to talk about death—their sadness, their worries, their fears. A courageous friend will not change the subject but will let the conversation reveal the feelings that are shared.

Eric Nelson, a high school senior, had a unique experience with death. He tells about it in the following account.

His Final Chapter

My parents and I arrived at the hospital about 2:00 a.m. The evening nurse greeted us and escorted us to my grandfather's room. The hospital was dim and was like an indoor cemetery, except the sounds of coughs and snores proved otherwise.

I was scared.

Only five months before, my grandpa had been diagnosed with cancer. Although the initial prognosis was good, he declined very quickly because the disease spread throughout his body. Despite his strength and his desire to live, the cancer was winning and he lapsed into a coma.

We entered his room and exchanged our "hellos" with the family. These weren't hellos that consisted of words, [but] rather tears and hugs. Like spokes, all of us took our places around Grandpa's bed as though he was the hub of our wheel. He was.

Glancing up after a prayer for my grandpa, I noticed that among my parents, aunts, uncles, and my grandma, I was the only child. I felt awkward at first. I wondered if the other adults felt I shouldn't have been there. Or were they jealous that their kids couldn't come. Rescuing me from my callous thinking, Uncle Don leaned over, grabbed my hand, and whispered, "Eric, though it doesn't seem so now, this will be a very special time in your life, and you will never forget this night."

Looking at my grandpa, I noticed his yellowish skin color, like that of an overly ripe pear. This was caused by the malfunction of the disease-infested liver. His feet and abdomen were swollen to twice their normal size. This, too, was an ill effect of that wretched cancer that was taking my grandpa away from me. I couldn't believe that a man who was so caring, whom I looked up to and respected, a man whom I loved so much, was dying. I wanted to help him so much. If I could only breathe for him.

I was crying.

I listened while everyone reminisced about Grandpa's accomplishments. He had been a Chevy dealer for eighteen years and was one of the nation's best insurance salesmen for eleven. They remembered his commitment to others and his philosophy of sharing his gifts with those around him. He demonstrated this by being very active in church and by teaching classes on insurance to younger salesmen. They talked about his greatest joy—collecting classic cars; and how he personalized each car with its individual name. It made me think of the rides I had taken with him in my favorite car, Phil, a baby blue '52 Chevy.

I was smiling.

The conversation drifted to "Grandpa stories." Uncle Dick told us how Grandpa, who drove the town tow truck, had to rescue him and his prom date when the car was up to the axles in mud. My mother mentioned the time Grandpa saved her dolls when they fell into the outhouse basement. Grandma recalled when he came home to relax once. Grandpa sat down in his easy chair and kicked off his shoes. His shoes went sailing, shattering the window.

I was laughing.

Grandpa's breathing began to weaken.

How lucky I was to be a part of his life. How fortunate I was to see the family share some of the chapters of his life. I not only knew *my* Grandpa, but through everyone's stories I knew *their* Grandpa, too. I wanted him to wake up so we could take him home. He wouldn't. I wanted to thank him for being my grandpa and letting me be here to see his final chapter. His dying wasn't all tragedy because this night he had given us the opportunity to share the joy he had given each of us.

His breaths were coming less frequently now. I found myself counting the seconds between each breath. Three seconds, twelve seconds, seventeen seconds. . . .

I was crying.

CHAPTER THREE

After Death, What?

We know what life is. It is made up of many things. To be alive is to see a sunrise, eat an ice cream cone, giggle, grumble, be happy, and be sad. But death is an unknown. That is what makes it scary. An old man who was dying said, "Death is a wall. I don't know what is on the other side."

Wondering about what is "on the other side" is as old as humankind. We realize that physical death is final. But people have always considered the possibility that each person has a soul, and that a spiritual life may go on. Webster's dictionary defines a soul as "the spirit of a dead person, thought of as separate from the body and leading an existence of its own." If a soul—a spirit—lives on, where does it go? If there is a life after death, what is it like?

There is evidence from their burial practices that an ancient group of people called Scythians believed that life after death would be very much like this one. Warriors were buried with the weapons they would need in their next life. A man's horse was killed and buried also. Thus the warrior would have a mount for future battles. A woman was buried with her personal belongings and sometimes with her cooking pots.

In her book *The Brothers Lionheart*, Swedish author Astrid Lindgren presented an idea of life after death in which two boys keep their bodies and go on to have adventures in a land called Nangiyala. Nangiyala is an exciting place. There one of the boys, Karl, who has been an invalid all his life, experiences the action he missed on earth. In this land of dragons, serpents, and evil, good triumphs and Karl finds courage. When their time in Nangiyala is over, the boys go on to another land and another life.

The idea of one life following another is embodied in another interesting concept: reincarnation.

Reincarnation

Funk and Wagnalls Encyclopedia explains that the belief in reincarnation is, in its simplest form, ''found in several tribes of Africa and America who think the soul at death must look out for a new host to inhabit, and if need be will enter the body of an animal.'' Two Eastern religions, Buddhism and Hinduism, also believe that death is not final but only one link in a chain of many lives.

Buddha, the founder of Buddhism, is said to have undergone 550 rebirths. These led to lives as a hermit, a king, a slave, an ape, an elephant, a fish, a frog, and a tree. Buddhists hope that they will be reborn to live a religious life. Finally, they may reach a state called nirvana and break out of the circle of death and rebirth to become one with all things.

Hindus, too, believe that they go through many lives, deaths, and rebirths. Death is to them a natural part of a great circle. For Hindus the idea of becoming one tiny part of the great force of the universe is wonderful.

Other religious beliefs

The idea of rebirth in another form exists in the Jewish, Christian, and Moslem religions also. But the forms are not clearly defined. Much depends on how one lived life on this earth. The Jewish religion teaches that the soul goes directly to God. Followers of this faith place great emphasis on living a good life and leaving the fate of the soul up to God.

Within Christianity there are two main groups—Protestants and Catholics. Protestants, of which there are many sects, generally feel

Reprinted from *Childhood Is Hell*, by Matt Groening. Courtesy of Pantheon Books, a division of Random House, Inc., NY

that if they have loved God, their spirits will dwell with God in heaven forever. Catholics emphasize God's love also, but regard eternal life as a reward for living up to religious standards and patterns of behavior.

Moslems believe that the good are rewarded and the wicked punished after death. Good people, according to Moslem teachings, go to paradise when they die. The wicked will live in hell forever.

Heaven and hell

It is an unusual person who has not wondered what heaven would be like. Or its opposite—hell.

The Catholic Religion—A Manual of Instruction for Members of the Anglican Church explains that "heaven is the place and the blessed condition of unending happiness in the Presence of God, and His holy angels and saints." It adds, "It consists also in an endless reunion with all we have loved below, who have died in grace, and in our being perfectly good and holy for evermore."

Some people are satisfied with this much information. Others want more detail. Thus, heaven has been depicted in popular movies and TV shows as a place where people sit on clouds playing harps, or

The belief in an afterlife of painful punishment has inspired the imagination of many an artist through the ages. This sixteenth-century German woodcut depicts Hell as a monstrous hound devouring the damned.

float endlessly, wearing white robes and smiling. To some people, this may not be an idea of bliss. But we can only imagine what heaven is like. The hope of being reunited with loved ones who have died can be a great comfort.

But what if you are condemned to hell? *The World Book Encyclopedia* says, "Hell, according to many religions, is a place or state inhabited by demons, where wicked people are punished after death." The belief in physical punishment after death has been abandoned by certain Protestant sects. And the nature of punishments in hell is controversial.

It can be argued that nobody is all good, or all bad. So who will go to heaven? Who to hell? *The Jewish Encyclopedia* answers these questions by saying:

> In the last judgment day there shall be three classes of souls: the righteous shall at once be written down for the life everlasting; the wicked, for Gehenna [hell]; but those whose virtues and sins counterbalance one another shall go down to Gehenna and float up and down until they rise purified.

In Catholic tradition, a similar place—between heaven and hell—is called purgatory.

Ancient people and their beliefs

In his book *The Final Mystery*, author Stanley Klein tells of two other cultures and their ways of thinking about death.

Klein says that less than fifty years ago the Lugbara tribe of east-central Africa believed that a person who died was no longer "of the world." He became a person "in the earth." His body was no more, and some part of him went to live somewhere beneath the ground. His soul, called the *orindi*, went into the sky. When a special person—an important leader of the tribe, for instance—died, his *orindi* returned to earth as a ghost. The family made sacrifices to the ghost, and the ghost felt special responsibility toward his relatives.

The Pygmies of central Africa did not believe in an afterlife. A person who was dead was just gone. Friends and relatives grieved and tried to return to normal life as soon as possible. Klein says, "Like the ancient Lugbara, the Pygmies are changing their old ways because they have met with the outside world."

Even nonreligious people feel the uniqueness of every human being. And although no one has proved beyond all doubt that a soul exists, most people persist in believing that something of the individual person continues to survive the experience of dying. But not all do.

Existentialists

Like the Pygmies, a group called existentialists believe that this life is all we have. Existentialism holds that each person exists as an individual in a purposeless universe. Those who embrace this philosophy feel that if life is to be joyful and have meaning, people must make it so and bring purpose to it themselves.

People like existentialists appear to be in the minority, judging from the numerous stories of afterlife that abound worldwide. Certainly the mystery of what is beyond death affects all of us. Consequently, it affects the way we treat life and death. Customs accompanying death are often overlaid with age-old traditions, and the manner in which we bury our dead and grieve over them reflects our beliefs as well as the beliefs of those around us.

No one is sure what happens to a person's spirit, if indeed such a thing exists, after death. But people do know what happens to the body. When life is gone from a body it changes color and muscles stiffen. Soon it decomposes (rots). Most often, before decomposition can take place, the body—or corpse, as it is also called—is put into a morgue. This is a refrigerator-like room kept cold enough so the corpse will not decompose. A hospital usually has such a room in the basement or other out-of-the-way place. The body is removed to a mortuary, or funeral home, as soon as possible. If the person died at home, the body is taken directly to the mortuary, which also has facilities for keeping bodies cold.

Doonesbury / By Garry Trudeau

In some cases an autopsy may be performed. In an autopsy, the body is cut open and its organs are examined by a doctor to find out exactly what caused the death. After the autopsy is completed, the body is sewed up. Editor Eric E. Rofes, in *The Kids' Book About Death and Dying*, explains that:

> The state has the right to ask for an autopsy to be performed when someone dies under certain circumstances that might be suspicious, involving such causes as violence, injuries at their workplace, malnutrition, drugs, or sexual abuse, or when a person dies suddenly and without obvious cause, or is simply found dead.

With some exceptions, such as criminal cases, doctors must get permission from the next of kin (closest relative of the dead person) before they can perform an autopsy. When the cause of death has been determined, a death certificate is made out. The body is then disposed of in whatever way the survivors designate. Usually the survivors decide to have the body preserved and buried or cremated.

Preservation

Historians believe that embalming (the art of preserving bodies after death) began with the Egyptians, probably before 4000 B.C. They injected the arteries and veins of the dead body with balsams (substances that flow from certain plants). Then they filled the cavities of the torso with fragrant substances and salt, and wound the body with cloths treated with similar materials. The Assyrians used honey in embalming; the Persians used wax.

Today, if a body is to be preserved it is taken to a funeral home. There all the blood is drained through a small incision in a vein. Then liquid chemicals are pumped into the body through the arteries and flushed through the blood vessels. The chemicals penetrate the tissues and preserve the body until burial. Embalming fluids come in various shades such as "Suntan" and "Moderately Pink." These are intended to make the corpse appear as lifelike as possible.

Ancient Egyptians embalm a corpse. Preserved food was often placed beside the body before burial to strengthen the deceased on his or her journey through the underworld.

When the body tissues have become firm and dry—in about eight to ten hours—the funeral director begins restorative work on the body. The director may clean the corpse's teeth or sew up the mouth. He or she combs the hair (or hires a hairdresser to do it) and shaves the face if there is a stubble of beard. Makeup is used to cover wounds or damaged body parts. A plaster ear, for example, may be made to replace one that was cut off in an accident.

In spite of the funeral director's best efforts, a body may not look the way the survivors remember the person when she was alive. When Pam described her grandmother's body at the funeral, she said, "She looked awful. She never wore that much makeup—and yet she looked all faded. Almost like wax. I could tell she was dead, all right. My aunt said Grandma looked peaceful. But I thought she just looked dead."

The purpose of burial

To some people the practice of embalming a body and putting it on display is distasteful. But it has become so common that embalming is often not questioned. Many people say that seeing the body assures them that the person is really dead. The casket does not have to be kept open for the funeral, but a body must be either kept cold or embalmed until it is buried or cremated. Otherwise it will begin to smell, and it may be a health hazard.

In the past, before refrigeration and embalming, a body buried in a simple wooden coffin would usually decompose in a year or two so only bones remained. Bodies then became part of the soil, contributing to the life cycle. This concept is illustrated in a children's book titled *Ten Good Things About Barney* by Judith Viorst. In this book a cat's body is buried in the backyard. It becomes part of the soil, thus acting as fertilizer so the flowers grow taller and stronger.

If a body is embalmed, placed in a casket, and then in an airtight vault, the body may last fifty years or more. The casket and vault may last decades longer. It will be a very long time before these things become part of the environment.

Mausoleums

Another common way today of disposing of a person's remains is to keep the body above ground, in a building called a mausoleum. The pyramids built by the ancient Egyptians are mausoleums where important people were buried.

Today mausoleums are being built to hold hundreds or even thousands of bodies. Vaults are built into the walls, like safety deposit boxes in banks. Embalmed bodies or the remains of those that are cremated may be kept there. Mausoleums save more space than cemeteries, and some people prefer to think of their bodies being kept in a place that is warm and dry rather than buried in the ground.

Bodies in a mausoleum, even though embalmed, eventually rot because of bacteria and mold. The odor is not apparent because the mausoleum is kept well-ventilated.

Cremation

Many ancient people believed that only fire could free the soul of a dead person. Cremating, or burning, is the second oldest form of disposing of a dead body. This practice is not as popular in the United States as it is in Eastern countries and in Europe. However, it is becoming more common. One reason is the fact that cremation is not as expensive as embalming and burial. A body that is going to be cremated does not have to be placed in a casket. It can be burned in a heavy cardboard box.

People who prefer cremation also think of it as a dignified means of disposing of the body. The Cremation Society of Minnesota says that many of its members "are concerned citizens who look toward the future and the eventual scarcity of land." They like the idea that cremated remains do not take up cemetery space.

The ashes and bone fragments left after the cremation process may be placed in an urn and given to the family to keep. They may also be scattered over private property. The Cremation Society of Minnesota says, ''Your cremated remains [ashes] will be handled according to your written instructions, or may be picked up by your survivors to do with as they wish, or will be delivered or mailed for a fee.''

Mark Stohlberg, a funeral director who also provides cremation services, believes that if ashes are scattered, it is important that the

Family members place flowers on the casket of the deceased before burial at a cemetery. In the U.S., burial has become the most common way of disposing of a deceased person's remains, but cremation is becoming an acceptable alternative.

place be designated in some way, perhaps with a plaque under a tree, or a memorial bench near the site. He believes people need a place to come to be near the deceased, so that they can think about the deceased person.

Observing appropriate customs

Human skeletons were discovered some years ago in mounds of empty clam shells found on the shores of some Japanese islands. The bones were in good condition after thousands of years because the chemical composition of the shells helped to preserve them. Archeologists who carefully removed the shells report that most of the skeletons were found in a similar position. They were lying curled up like a baby being carried inside its mother's body. Some of the skeletons had stones resting on their chests. Some lay in the center of a circle of stones, and some skeletons were painted red.

The scientists believe that the painted bodies must have been buried twice, so that the flesh could rot off the bones before they were painted. (If the bodies had been left to decompose without burial the smell would have been unbearable.) Just what preceded the burial, we may never know, because these people left no written records. But the evidence indicates that, like the Scythians who buried weapons with their warriors, these people had rituals that accompanied the event of death. ''Rituals link us with the past and future,'' explains Dr. Judith Stillion, a professor of psychology at Western Carolina University. They also honor the dead and provide a measure of comfort to the survivors.

In Western society we often call such rituals, customs. These customs include condolence calls, funerals, and memorials as means of dealing with death.

Condolence call sounds more formal than it really is. A condolence call is merely a visit to the home of the family of the deceased. It is made as soon as possible after the news of a death has reached friends and relatives. Neighbors may come with food, knowing that no one in the family feels like cooking. Or they offer to perform a service, such as taking care of young children while the adults are busy and possibly overcome with shock or grief. The presence of other people makes the survivors feel less alone. Having visitors also gives the family a chance to discuss the details of the death. During the course of these conversations the mourners learn that others care and understand what they are going through. "It doesn't matter what you say," explained a grief counselor. "The important thing is that you *be* there."

Funerals

If funeral arrangements have not been made beforehand—and many times they have—decisions must be made as to what will happen next. Will a mortuary, or funeral home, take care of the body and the funeral service? Will the body be displayed? Will it be buried in the traditional manner, or cremated? What are the wishes of the family? There is much to be handled in the days following death. It is easier if the deceased has expressed some thoughts as to what they prefer. These thoughts are usually honored by the survivors, but the living also have a right to express their wishes. Many people argue that the funeral is not for the dead, but for the survivors, because the corpse can no longer see, feel, or hear what is happening.

When funeral plans have been made, newspapers often will publish an announcement called an obituary. If the deceased was a prominent citizen, or her death was considered newsworthy in some other way, the newspaper may publish a photograph and eight or ten paragraphs about her life, her accomplishments, and perhaps the organizations to which she belonged. However, if Uncle Harry, for instance, lived a quiet life, the newspaper, as a public service, may offer to print his name, age, address, and when and where his funeral will take place. The family may buy additional space to include the names of survivors and other information they feel will be of interest.

Here is a typical obituary:

JOHNSON

Oscar H., age 90 of Exeter Nursing
Home. Former resident of Boston
and Newark. For 36 years operated
Johnson Brothers Mobile Park, Boston. Member of Irwin Assleson Le-
gion Post, Newark, Masonic Lodge,
Scottish Rite & Shrine. Survived by
daughter Shirley Vanzo, Pueblo, CO;
son Alan, Newark; eight grand-
children; 10 great-grandchildren;
brothers Vilas & Gus. Funeral services 2 pm Wed. Reviewal 6-8 pm
Tues. at Riestad Funeral Home, Boston. Private interment Jones Lake
Cemetery. Memorials preferred to
the Shriner's Hospital for Crippled
Children.

The reviewal is sometimes called a visitation. It is similar to a condolence call, but it takes place in the funeral home or in the church
before the funeral service. This is a time when the body is present,
clothed in garments chosen by the family and brought to the funeral
home to complete the funeral director's restoration. For a period of
from two to five hours, those who want to may walk past the coffin,
kneel before it to say a prayer, or stand near it for a silent good-bye.
In the past it was customary to touch the corpse, and some people
still do, but this can be frightening, especially to children. A fifty-
year-old man still remembers what that was like. He said, "I was
ten years old when my grandmother died. My mother made me kiss
Grandma as she lay in the coffin. It's the only thing I remember
about the funeral. It was terrible."

Reviewals are a custom in Christian funeral rites, but each religion
has its own way of dealing with death.

Protestant funeral services usually include a scripture lesson from the Bible, prayers, a short sermon, and group readings or singing of hymns. There is no set form. A Catholic ceremony is similar, but a formal Mass is included. The services become more meaningful to many people when individuals participate by speaking about the deceased, singing his favorite songs, or perhaps playing his favorite instrument. A Protestant funeral rarely lasts more than twenty-five or thirty minutes; a Catholic one with a Mass lasts closer to an hour.

Some people attend only the reviewal but not the funeral. They may not be able to get time off from work to attend the services, usually held during the day.

Police officials present a memorial plaque to the family of a boy who had been an honorary member of the police force before he died of a terminal illness.

Daytime funerals may be more of a practical consideration than part of a ritual, since burial often follows the funeral services, and cemeteries are not lit at night. The cars that follow the hearse to the cemetery turn their headlights on as a way of showing passersby that this is no ordinary string of cars. Sometimes tiny flags are placed on the hoods of the cars, and a police escort may accompany the funeral procession. When one comes upon such a line of cars the proper procedure is to stop and wait quietly until the procession passes.

Another brief service may be conducted at the graveside. Mourners may watch while the casket is lowered into the grave or choose to leave before this is done.

A memorial service

Occasionally another type of observance, called a memorial service, is held. It is similar to a regular funeral except that the body is not present. A soldier who died in battle and whose body may have been buried in another country might have a memorial service rather than a funeral. If a body has been cremated or donated to science, a memorial service is appropriate also. Another example is a case in which a person retired and moved to another area. The friends where he lived for most of his life may mark his death by a memorial service.

Jewish funerals

Orthodox Jews conform to established religious doctrine and have special ways of handling death. Their ceremonies are simple ones. Strict Jewish law does not permit embalming, but the dead person is washed and placed in a white shroud or burial garment. If possible, the dead person is buried the following day. In the Jewish tradition there is no coffin, but if the laws of the country say that coffins must be used, those laws will be followed.

Special prayers are said at home before the funeral, at the funeral home, or at the grave. These prayers praise life and affirm that a life was lived. Traditionally, Jews remain at home for seven days after the funeral of a family member. This seven-day mourning period is called *shivah*. During this time relatives and friends visit to offer their support. Some families may attend services every day for the next year to commemorate the deceased.

Funeral customs of Eastern religions

Like those of Christians and Jews, Moslem funeral customs are not rigidly structured but adapt to local laws and customs. The family is supposed to take care of all the details of the funeral. The body is washed and wrapped in linen, placed in a simple wooden coffin, and carried to the service. The service is held in a Moslem temple or in an open space near the person's home. Few people attend the burial. At the grave, the body is taken from the coffin and gently placed in the earth, facing Mecca, the Moslem holy city. Moslems believe that the dead can feel pain, so they are never cremated.

Hindus, on the other hand, place their dead on a funeral pyre, which is a heap of material for burning. After a short ceremony the body is smeared with a sacred butter called *ghee*. Then a close relative lights the pyre while members of the family march around it. Three days after the cremation, whatever bones have not been consumed by the fire are collected and placed in a vase. These remains are then tossed into the nearest body of water, because Hindus believe that all waters flow into the sacred Ganges River. More ceremonies follow to ensure that the soul will get a new body and be reborn.

Like Hindus, Buddhists believe that death is not final. The dead must, however, travel for forty-nine days through *bardo*, between death and rebirth. For three days Buddhist priests stay with the dead and chant to send the soul on its way. A feast is held, and then a funeral band of three men is formed. The three go alone to the burial place. But the family must perform ceremonies for the full forty-nine days.

They offer special prayers and pay the priests who are helping them. After forty-nine days, the ceremonies are over and the soul is ready to be reborn.

Personal preferences

What if a family belongs to no religious faith? And what if they cannot afford a traditional funeral involving a mortuary? Or what if they want to depart from tradition for other reasons?

There can be many variations when it comes to planning a funeral. A service may be held on a mountaintop or in a field. A body may be buried at sea. A man who loved to sail asked that his body be embalmed, placed aboard his yacht, and towed out to deep water. There, he said, he wanted the boat sunk, with him aboard. His wishes were carried out.

In his book *Endings*, Buff Bradley tells of a group of friends who took care of everything when a young man named Luke died. They asked the hospital to keep his body in the morgue until they could make plans. They filed a death certificate at the county courthouse to make everything legal. They checked the local laws, then designed and built Luke's coffin with loving care. When it was ready they put Luke's body in it, put the coffin in the back of an old school bus, and rode with Luke to a nearby cemetery where he was cremated.

A memorial service was held at Luke's school. During the service, a tape of Luke playing music he had written was a touching part of the ceremony. Someone who was there described it as "a celebration of a young man's life."

Gravestones—monuments to the dead

The places where bodies are buried are special places. They are marked in some way. A common way is to place a gravestone over the grave.

One need only walk through a cemetery to see the variety of gravestones put up by grieving survivors. They are, as *Webster's Dic-*

Graves are typically marked with a headstone containing dates of birth and death and sometimes an epitaph. A cemetery in Long Island, New York is pictured here.

tionary says, "erected over a grave to preserve the memory of the deceased." They may be plain or highly decorated, large or small. They may contain only a name and dates of birth and death, or they may contain an epitaph, designed to express in a few words something about the person's life.

Some use more than a few words. For example, an epitaph written for Benjamin Franklin, American diplomat, inventor, and printer reads:

BENJAMIN FRANKLIN, 1706-1790
The body of
B. Franklin,
Printer;
Like the cover of an old Book,
Its contents torn out,
And stript of its Lettering and Gilding,
Lies here, Food for Worms.
But the Work shall not be wholly lost;
For it will, as he believ'd, appear once more,
In a new and more perfect Edition,
Corrected and amended
By the Author.
He was born Jan. 6, 1706.
Died 17-

In contrast, the epitaph for American inventor Alexander Graham Bell is simply:

So little done, so much to do.

And from a Vermont cemetery comes an epitaph in a humorous vein:

Here lies
the body of our Anna
Done to death
by a banana.
It wasn't the fruit
that laid her low
But the skin of the thing
that made her go.

Feelings about funerals

Even though funerals are a common part of American culture, it is common for people to avoid going to them. Some people feel like Kent did when his friend's father died:

"Do I *have* to go to the funeral?" Kent asked his mother. "Funerals are awful. Nobody will care if I don't go."

At the frown on his mother's face, Kent tried another tactic: "I don't even have a black suit to wear."

"You don't need a black suit. People don't always wear black like they used to. Wear what you'd wear to church, or to a meeting where you'd like to make a good impression."

"But what will I say?"

"Just say, 'I'm sorry about your dad.'"

"Is that all?"

"Yes. The important thing is that you go. And take a handkerchief."

Kent went, wore dress pants and a sweater, met friends, and later said he was glad he had gone to the funeral. "I felt so sorry for Bill I had to wipe away a tear," Kent said.

The fear of showing emotion in public is one of the strongest reasons people dislike going to funerals. But "Crying is a means by which people acknowledge the death of a loved one and work their way out of despair," says a funeral director. "Tears are not evidence of weakness. Weeping can be a shared experience." This funeral director agreed with Kent's mother, that it is important to go. "You help the bereaved when you attend the funeral. Being there demonstrates that although someone has died, friends like you still remain. 'Being there' is an eloquent statement that you care."

Funerals do not have to be all sad. The coming together of people who have not seen each other for a long time can bring a lighter note to the day. Usually refreshments are served afterwards, in the church hall, or at a home. "When my aunt died we all went to my cousin's house afterwards," said Mary. "I didn't know how I was supposed to act, but we had lunch, and everyone stood around and talked. Some people were laughing. It didn't seem right to me to be having fun when Aunt Agnes was dead, but my dad said it was okay. He thought Aunt Agnes wouldn't mind, she'd want us to enjoy the family reunion even if she wouldn't be there."

The funeral industry

A typical funeral—the kind with embalming, a satin-lined casket, limousine service to the cemetery, and so forth—can cost thousands of dollars. Prices vary throughout the United States, but in 1989 a total of three thousand to five thousand dollars was a reasonable estimate. The funeral industry has often been criticized for charging too much for its services. In some cases this may be true, but since 1963, when a book called *The American Way of Death* was published, the industry has been very careful in its dealings with the public. In this book, author Jessica Mitford accused funeral directors of taking advantage of people too grief-stricken to think clearly, and of profiting from their sorrow. Since then, caskets in all price ranges are usually displayed. Also, an itemized list of services (such as getting the death certificate signed, cost of the visitation room, and embalming) is gone over with the family. In the book *Coping with Dying*, Dr. Robert Raab says, "In my own experience, I have found most funeral directors to be sympathetic and helpful to the mourners."

Whether the bones are painted red, or the body is placed in a silk-lined casket, the rituals of death are necessary. They help the living say good-bye to the dead and prepare to move on with their lives. Feelings about death do not end with the funeral. A death changes many things for many people. A business will have to find a new manager, a school a new teacher. But it is those who were close to the deceased who will feel the loss most deeply, and for a long period of time.

CHAPTER FOUR

Surviving a Loss: Grieving

Eleven-year-old Jeanne Marie had her first experience with death when her dog Maggie was hit by a car. Maggie bounded out of the house, eager for a morning run. Jeanne Marie followed, but before she could get Maggie under control a car came careening around a curve. There was a screech of brakes. Jeanne Marie screamed. Maggie lay dying in the dew-covered grass by the side of the road.

"For a while I just stared at Maggie, and I couldn't stop screaming," Jeanne Marie remembers. "Then I cried and cried." What Jeanne Marie felt was grief, the deep sadness that follows a loss. When death tears a person's world apart, grieving is the process that helps put it back together.

Those who study death and dying say that grief follows a relatively predictable pattern. The stages of grief are not too unlike those experienced by people who find out they are dying. The first reaction is usually shock. This stage may last for days or weeks. This is a period when the survivors do not want to believe the friend or loved one is really dead. "No," they say. "It can't be true. He's not dead. It's a mistake. It happened to someone else."

Gradually the numbness of the first stage lessens, and the real pain of the loss is felt. This is when grief is felt most strongly. Finally the bereaved begin to adjust to living without the deceased. They find new interests and activities, and are able to go on with life. This whole process is called grief work by some psychologists. They look at grief as a series of tasks that must be worked through.

Different kinds of grief

Not everyone reacts in the same way, however, and the stages overlap. It is hard to shake those first feelings of shock and denial. They act as a sort of insulation, protecting the bereaved so they can manage to participate in the services and respond to expressions of sympathy from neighbors and friends. It is common for a person in the first phases of grief to have physical symptoms. Grief can feel like a great heaviness in your stomach. Or a terrible emptiness. It can make your throat tight. It can keep you from sleeping at night. People who have suffered intense grief say they sometimes felt like crying uncontrollably, or laughing when things were not really funny. People who are grieving have to have patience with themselves. It helps to know that the feelings are natural, and that they are not going crazy. Grief counselors say that if a person was not crazy before the death of a loved one, she is not going crazy now.

Buff Bradley in *Endings* says:

> When you feel grief, it isn't for the dead person, it's for your own loss and loneliness. Sometimes people make themselves feel worse by thinking it's selfish to feel so bad just because they miss someone who's gone—after all, the dead person isn't feeling any pain or suffering. The fact is, it's no more selfish to feel the pain of grief than it is to feel the pain of a broken bone. Would you call yourself selfish if you felt pain when you broke an arm? The pain of grief is as natural and unselfish as that.

When you lose someone you love, weird things can happen. Tom, a student in a class talking about death, said he was glad to hear that. "I thought I saw my dad in the mall one day," he confessed. "But I knew it wasn't really him. I know he's really dead." Gerald Koocher, an associate professor of psychology, explains that lots of people have similar experiences. Often they hear the voice of the dead person, or think they do. A woman whose husband had died said, "When I scratched the car, I *felt* his presence—I knew he was frowning at me—wherever he was!"

Sadness, anger, and guilt

People react to bereavement in a variety of ways. Right along with the deep sadness are feelings of anger and guilt. Sometimes the anger is directed at the dead person. "How could you do this to me?" the grief-stricken wails. "We had so many plans!" A high school teacher who was asked to teach a unit of death hesitated to approach the subject. But she did, and discovered that the anger she felt at her father for dying when she was a sophomore in high school had been hidden for years.

It does not seem fair to have someone you love die and leave you. You have the right to be angry. And fearful.

If someone your age dies—a friend perhaps—could you die too? It is a fear that is often unspoken, but it is there.

Guilt feelings are common, too. A five-year-old wonders, "Did Grandma die because of something I did?" Some people, young or old, feel that death is a kind of punishment. An older child may think, "If only I had been nicer to Grandma. I didn't go to visit her as

For Better or For Worse / By Lynn Johnston

often as I could have." Adults might try to reassure him that Grandma did not die because of his neglect, but he feels guilty anyway.

Even those who are not family may be affected by guilt for a long period of time. Jim was twenty-five when a college acquaintance jumped off a bridge to his death. Three years later Jim says, "I still think about it. I wonder if there was something I could have done . . . something I could have said." Feelings of guilt are especially strong for those left behind when someone takes his own life.

Sadness and loss

When the reality of death sinks in, the sadness and loss may be overwhelming. Then even a normally happy, capable person can become gloomy and dull and feel that nothing matters. This is a state of depression that usually decreases as the bereaved person works through the emotions of mourning.

"The feelings of grief last far longer than society in general allows," says author Nancy O'Connor in *Letting Go with Love*. Even close friends may expect us to be back to "normal" in a few weeks after a death. "But living with loss is not so simple. The death of someone close may cause emotional pain and confusion for months or even years," O'Connor believes.

A study done by the Institute of Medicine of the National Academy of Sciences concludes that a survivor's way of life is commonly disturbed for at least one year but may be affected for as long as three years. Psychologist Stephen Goldstone agrees there is no strict timetable for grieving. He says sadness may flare up on birthdays, wedding anniversaries, or other significant dates. Holidays are especially painful for many people after the death of a loved one.

A man whose wife has been dead for fifteen years said, "You really don't ever 'get over' it; you get used to it."

Though psychologists have studied grief to the extent that they see it in stages, more study is being done by mental health researchers to redefine normal grieving behavior. They are concerned with those who do not seem to be moving through the grieving process to a stage called resolution. It is difficult to know what behavioral signs among the bereaved signal a need for special help. People have different ways of coping with the pain they feel.

Counselor Stephen Levine believes that people need to grieve openly. "Let your heart break," he says. This means giving in to the tears, sharing the pain. But Norman Klein, an associate professor of anthropology, says some people can work through grief internally or privately. He cites Japanese-Americans as a group who do not like to show grief in public. Klein stresses that attitudes—and behavior—are clearly influenced by culture and individual personality. "It follows then, that we must take care not to formalize or prescribe the way in which people express emotion."

Some people prefer to grieve quietly and alone.

A death in the family

When we hear in the news of the death of a famous person we may feel sad that he or she will no longer enhance our world. When the relative of a friend dies we feel sad for the friend. But these deaths do not affect us in the same way that the death of someone close to us does. Each special death brings with it its own adjustment.

To some people, a dog, a cat, or a bird is like a member of the family. It is loved and cared for, and it lives with us, sometimes for many years. When it dies, the survivors, like Jeanne Marie, go through the emotions of grieving. Many families conduct funerals for pets, inventing rituals and imitating actual funeral procedures. The death and burial of a pet can serve as a preparation for deaths that follow later in life. The occasion can be a chance for children to ask questions and get answers about death.

Some people, especially those who live alone, are more attached to their pets than they are to other people. They may choose to bury their pets in the backyard, or in a pet cemetery, complete with a headstone. Rather than being "silly," such care in the disposal of a pet's body may be a vital step in the owner's grief process.

The death of an aging relative

The death of a grandparent is often the first loss of human life that is felt keenly. If the older relative lived far away and visited only on occasion, the loss will be felt differently than if there was day-to-day contact. In the first case there may be a trip to the funeral, and a period of time when the family must "settle the affairs" of the deceased, putting away belongings, perhaps selling a house. Then life goes on much as it had before.

Elderly residents of a nursing home pass the time with a game of bingo. The often slow decline of the elderly toward death allows their relatives to prepare for the inevitable parting and grieving.

If the grandparent had been very ill, perhaps in a nursing home for many months, the death may come as a relief for everyone. It is true that some old people welcome death. The survivors may feel thankful that the deceased will no longer feel pain. They have been grieving for a long time in anticipation of their loss.

This is what happened when Peggy's grandmother died: "Nana had been in a nursing home for eleven years," said the thirteen-year-old. "When my mother and I went to visit her we never knew what to expect. Sometimes Nana recognized us and sometimes she asked who we were! Sometimes she scolded us for no reason, or said funny things like, 'Have you peeled the potatoes yet?' It was as if she was already gone, in a way. It made us feel so bad, we cried all the way home in the car. When she had a heart attack and died I think we had cried so much we didn't need to anymore."

The same sort of reaction may occur in any death that has been prolonged. One need not feel guilty about experiencing relief.

When a sibling dies

In the book *The Stone Pony* by Patricia Calvert, JoBeth suffers the loss of her sister Ashley. Ashley had much to live for—she was pretty and popular and won blue ribbons in riding shows. "Why couldn't it have been me?" JoBeth asks. Such questions are common when a sister or brother dies. The remaining children feel guilty just for being alive. Another question may arise to haunt the siblings also: "If she died, could I die too?" If the cause of death was an illness, it is only natural to worry that the same disease may strike again. A visit to a doctor will help to erase that concern.

When the initial stages of grief have been worked through, what remains is called secondary grief. It is felt when routines change. Someone else will have to take out the garbage. There may be only one child now to wash the dishes. There is bound to be resentment at some of the changes, as well as sadness at the loss. In addition, parents are so overwhelmed with the death of the child they may forget to give needed attention to the remaining children. Or, in contrast, they may be overprotective of their other children.

Joe's brother died in a skiing accident. Now his parents do not want Joe to join the ski team. Such reactions delay the family's return to normal living. Discussion groups formed for families can get fears out into the open so they can be discussed. Ways can be found for dealing with these fears.

It is a sad fact that friends may not know how to be helpful even if they want to be sympathetic and show that they care. They may withdraw, or act as if nothing has happened. It may be up to the grieving person to start a conversation to lessen the tension. If this is not done some people will never feel comfortable enough to talk about

A young family visits together outside the hospital where the child is being treated for leukemia. The mystery of death seems even deeper and more difficult to understand when a child dies and so the grieving process may continue longer.

the death with the survivor. As a result friendships may be altered. It is difficult to feel close to someone who ignores an important event in your life.

The death of a parent

No one knows how it feels to have a parent die unless it has happened to him or her. Realizing this, author Jill Krementz interviewed eighteen children who had suffered this terrible loss. She wrote *How It Feels When a Parent Dies* so that others may know that their anguish and guilt, confusion and anger are shared by others who understand. Krementz says, "Of course there can be no easy or simple comfort for the pain of a parent's death. But we all know how emotionally helpful it can be to realize that others have felt some of the same things we are feeling." She adds, "Often a child whose parent has died doesn't know anyone else this has happened to, and feels particularly isolated and 'special' in a very distressing way."

For more than one of the children Krementz interviewed, it was embarrassing to go back to school. They felt as if they were in a world of their own. Some wanted to talk about their parent's death to their friends. Others did not, because it made them so sad they wanted to change the subject.

Children's feelings

Here are some of the feelings that the children shared in Jill Krementz's book:

> Jack, whose father died, says, "I don't really talk about my father very much. I talk to my mother once in a while, but I usually keep my feelings to myself. I don't want my mother to start crying because if she starts crying she starts coughing and stuff. . . . She's had kidney stones about four times . . . so I worry that her kidney stones are going to get worse and worse and the next thing you know—pop! There she goes too."
>
> Susan's mother died when she was six. At thirteen Susan said,

"When someone dies, they're considered perfect because you don't really want to remember the bad things—only the good. . . . I don't want to remember any bad things about my mom."

Laurie's father had been dead only two months when she talked to Jill Krementz. Laurie said, "In some ways it's easier for me that my father died the way he did [in a plane crash]—all of a sudden—instead of having to go through a lot of pain and suffering. The way I think of it is that someone good came down and picked him up because it was his time." Then Laurie added, "But it's still hard for me to believe it's really happened. Sometimes when I'm reading a book I'll forget and then all of a sudden I stop and remember."

Nick, at age fifteen, said, "The thing about losing a mother is that now I know I can take just about anything. It was so painful, but I survived the loss and it's made me a stronger person."

Eda J. LeShan, author of *Learning to Say Good-by: When a Parent Dies*, says, "Losing a parent is the worst thing that can happen to a child."

For some people, writing about feelings is easier than talking about them. One high school senior wrote the following entry in his journal:

Silence in the Heart
by Mark Prebonich

Last year seems just like yesterday. I was struggling to be a man. I wanted the responsibilities of an adult, yet I enjoyed being a child. I still liked to do immature things such as hanging half naked, upside down from a tree, howling like a wounded hyena. Those were the best years of my life.

Over the past couple of years, the relationship between my father and me had taken off like a rocket. Believe me, there is no place I would rather be than fishing in Canada with my father; and every second spent in the boat with him was more precious to me than gold. We belonged together. I remembered this feeling on last year's fishing trip.

I awoke to the cool, crisp air of the Canadian wilderness. My body tingled as I stumbled out of my bunk. I quickly jumped into the same clothes that I had been wearing for the past three days and ran to the door of our primitive little cabin. The first few rays of the sun were just beginning to shed their warmth on the day. Walking out of the cabin, I noticed a fine mist rising off of the gently flowing river. My father was already in the boat. I quickly turned around to snatch up my rod and heard the familiar cry, "Let's! . . . Go! . . . Fishing! . . ."

We fished that whole day, nonstop, and caught walleye after walleye. It was, by far, the best trip we ever had. The sun never seemed to set as fast as it did that day. Everything was perfect. There was a twinkle in my father's eye that told me so. Softly, he said, "Wouldn't it be nice to end on a double?" I agreed. Darkness crept over the water and a nip was now present in the air. We decided to make our last casts. "I got one," I yelled as the tip of my rod bent toward the water. I turned toward my father as I wrestled the fish. He had a grin from ear to ear. He had one on his line too. "It's a double!" he roared. There couldn't be a more ideal ending to a perfect trip. Tomorrow we would leave.

I still remember that trip. It sticks in my mind as if only yesterday we were in that paradise of nature. I still remembered it as I was driving home from a comedy club late one Friday night.

The flashing of red lights was the first thing I noticed as my car came over the hill next to my house. My senses were numbed by the pulsing lights, which seemed to be in rhythm with the rapid beating of my heart. A great emptiness flooded my body. Oh God, oh God, please don't let this be for my house. But it was. I swallowed my stomach and wearily walked to the door. Furniture had been tossed aside and I could hear a great commotion going on in my parents' bedroom. Paramedics were rushing about like bees in a frenzy. My sister was standing petrified at the top of the stairs. "It's Dad," she whispered in a shaky voice. One small policeman said, "Good luck, son. It doesn't look good."

The smell of the hospital was overwhelming as my mother, sister, and I walked through the automated doors into the emergency wing. I was enveloped by a dull and dreary atmosphere as we were led into a small waiting room. The soft click of the closing door rang in my ears, almost deafening. My senses had abandoned me and the pit in my stomach grew as I sat there for what seemed to be an eternity. Time stood still. I felt myself outside of my body, watching my body. Seconds turned into minutes and minutes turned into hours. Not one muscle in my body moved. The door to our little prison finally creaked open as a doctor walked in. Technical terms flowed out of his mouth as do excuses out of a boy who's just broken his mother's best china vase. Not one thing he said mattered. None, except one soul-wrenching phrase, "We did everything we could."

I expected tears to come to my eyes like water from a broken water main but none did. I felt as if I was in shock. Walking out of the hospital, the realization finally hit me. It was then that the tears found their way out. I knew my life would never be the same.

It is easy to want to be older when there is a choice. There is always an innocence to fall back upon. I feel like I have been reduced to an infant and thrown to the tigers, thrown to the role of being an adult in an adult world. Not wanting to be, but having to be, and feeling, I'm not ready to be an adult yet. But I am.

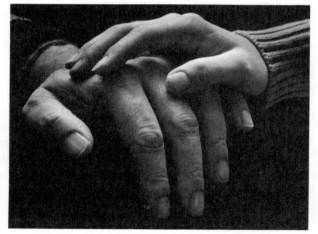

Often the best consolation to offer a grieving person is a silent touch that shows you share his or her pain without trying to take it away.

For a young person, losing a parent is a difficult adjustment. Joanne E. Bernstein, who wrote *Loss and How to Cope with It*, says, "You may have noticed that before your mother or father died, most or all of your friends had two parents. Now you seem to be picking up youngsters from broken homes, one after another. . . . It might be happening because, right now, you are uncomfortable in homes with two parents." Bernstein says it may be painful to watch a married couple talking together, laughing, or helping their child with homework. These are reminders of what is now missing in the bereaved person's life.

A friend from a single-parent home may be more understanding of feelings of loss, having experienced some similar ones through death or divorce. Bernstein advises that this shift in friendships is not something to worry about. It happens frequently to adults as well.

Some families fall into the habit of treating each other as replacements for the dead person. As an example, Bernstein cites Becky, who was the oldest child in the family. After her mother died Becky took over the shopping, cooking, and cleaning while trying to keep up with her school work. Becky was trying to take her mother's place in the household. This type of replacement can be a heavy burden for a young person.

Children and adult loneliness

Bernstein also has some advice for a young person who is asked to spend the night in the bed of the surviving parent. She says:

> Little and not-so-little boys may be asked to comfort their lonely mothers, and small and older girls may be asked to help their fathers feel better. Despairing parents may press for sexual contact with their children. It is sad that an adult is lonely; you may feel very sorry for your mother or father and want to give physical solace. Sharing a bed is not a good solution for the problem of loneliness. Young people belong in their own beds, as do all parents. If you are having trouble with a parent who insists, talk to another adult about the problem immediately.

Eventually, other people may enter the young person's life, and that of the remaining parent. These will not be replacements, but they will share some of the things that are missing in the survivors' lives. For instance, Susie found a Big Sister through a program designed to match up adults and children with similar interests. They go shopping and to lunch, something Susie and her mother used to do. In addition, they are both learning to ice-skate.

The surviving parent eventually may plan to remarry. This will mean more adjustments. The family will be "whole" again, but at the same time the stepparent is often seen as an intruder. A child may resent having some of his newly acquired responsibilities taken away from him. "My dad doesn't ask me to stop for milk after school anymore. My stepmother does that now," said Martin. "And she says I don't have to make my bed—she'll do that. But I didn't mind doing those things, and I resent her sometimes. It's nice to have her there when I come home—she bakes cookies, and things—but she'll never be 'Mom' to me. I call her Alice, like Dad does."

Having a stepparent is not the unusual situation it once was. Divorce is more common than in the past, people remarry, and the mean stepmothers of the fairy tales are just that—fairy tales. It often takes time for a re-formed family to feel natural, but it can be done, and it is done more often than not.

The death of a friend

The death of a friend may be as deeply disturbing as the death of a relative. With it comes the reminder that if someone your age can die, you can too. But apart from that is the change that such a death may make in your daily life. Along with the normal stages of grief comes secondary grief: "Who will I eat lunch with now?" wondered Mary when her friend was killed. She knew that she would make new friends, but for the moment, that did not help.

The death of a friend changes the lives of his or her companions. It can be very sad.

A woman tearfully remembers a loved one who has died. Grieving can recur when an external event, like a birthday, reminds one of the deceased.

Dr. Fred Neal, professor emeritus of religion at Rhodes College in Memphis, Tennessee, says, "There are two basic elements to grief—handling your own and helping others with theirs." Neal says those who reach out to the grieving may be rebuffed, but should not take it personally. When those who want to comfort say, "If there is anything I can do, let me know," the grief-stricken are so stunned by what has happened, they don't know what they need or want.

Here are some concrete suggestions based on Dr. Neal's advice:

1. *Be there.* Telephone. Ask if you can visit. A press of a hand, a hug, a few words of affection may be all that is needed.
2. *Listen.* A high school senior said, "Nobody wants to hear about my grandfather's death, and he was so important to me, I want to talk about it."
3. *Send a note.* It can be as simple as "I'm thinking of you during these painful days." A personal note is better than a sympathy card, but a printed card is better than no note.

4. *Give a gift.* A flower. A book. A sixth-grader brought a huge candy bar to her friend whose brother had died. "I'd heard that chocolate is comforting," she said.
5. *Extend an invitation.* Ask him to a hockey game. Take him to lunch. An invitation gives the bereaved something to look forward to—instead of only looking back on the source of his pain and suffering. Sometimes a grieving person will say no. They feel that if they have a good time they are being disloyal to the dead person's memory. Gentle encouragement will let them know it is alright to begin enjoying life again.

Grief counselors caution that one should not say "I know how you feel" unless they have gone through a similar experience and really do know. Then sharing your experience can be helpful.

Perhaps the best advice of all is *Be yourself.* Show concern and sorrow in your own way. Keep in touch. Be available.

Help for grieving children

"I am two people . . .the one other people see and the one who feels," says author Anne M. Brooks in *The Grieving Time.* Brooks writes from the perspective of a wife whose husband has died. But what she says applies also to children, who have been called the "forgotten grievers."

In their attempts to protect children from sadness, adults sometimes send children to visit a friend or a relative when a death occurs in the family, sometimes they are so absorbed in their own grief that they are emotionally unavailable to their children.

Marge Heegaard, program director at the National Childhood Grief Institute, says, "A child's grief may not be recognized because children express grief more in behavior than in words. . . .They tend to act out their anger and fear aggressively." Heegaard advises adults to tell it like it is, using terms like "die" and "dead" instead of phrases such as he's "having a long sleep," or she's "gone away."

"Do not exclude children when family or friends come to comfort grieving adults," Heegaard continues. "Avoidance or silence teaches children that death is a taboo subject. Children need to learn to cope with loss, not be protected from grief."

Dr. Barry Garfinkel, child psychiatrist at the University of Minnesota, believes children should be taken to wakes, funerals, reviewals, and burials, unless they object. An exception may be if the child would see a body badly marred by a traffic accident or some other trauma.

Yvonne Williams, M.S., a bereavement counselor, suggests making a treasure box as one way of helping a child work through grief. This may be a shoe box decorated by the child. Into it go reminders of the beloved person who has died. Written notes, pictures drawn by the child, photos, and small souvenirs of past good times are all appropriate. The box may be opened from time to time to be sorted through, giving the bereaved child a chance to talk or recall treasured memories.

The point grief counselors emphasize is that however it is handled, a child's grief should not be overlooked.

Tom Stocke, a Minnesota student, wrote a poem that poignantly applies to grief. It says in part:

> The silent cry of the young
> is hardly ever heard. . . .
> Only the young know
> what it is.
> The silent cry that is
> the pain that they go through. . . .

CHAPTER FIVE

Some Controversial Issues

Not everyone has the same feelings about death, life after death, funerals, and burials. Even though differences exist, people generally respect one another's beliefs. However, there are some topics connected with death that people feel so strongly about that their mere mention can bring on lively discussions at any gathering. These topics all involve death on purpose, the opposite of all our efforts to prevent death.

Arguments revolve around the question, are there ever good reasons for killing human beings? Some people think that under certain circumstances it might be kinder, more practical, or better for society, to cause death deliberately. Others feel that it is never right to take a human life.

Euthanasia

Euthanasia, killing an individual as an act of mercy, was discussed by Alan L. Otten in an article in *The Wall Street Journal*. He starts his article with a comparison from his own experiences.

> When I was a boy, my family had a beloved bulldog. Eventually he became very old—blind, incontinent, wheezing heavily, barely able to eat or walk. We took him to the vet and, as the euphemism then had it, the vet "put Jerry to sleep."

> Every few days now, I go to visit my 90-year-old mother in a nearby nursing home. She lies on her side in bed, legs drawn rigidly into a fetal position, blinks at me uncomprehendingly as I prattle on about family doings, and rarely utters a sound except a shriek of pain when the attendants turn her from one side to the other in their constant battle to heal her horrible bedsores. She must be hand-fed, and her incontinency requires a urethral catheter.

Otten goes on in detail describing his mother's condition, then asks, "Why do we treat our aged and loved animals better than we treat our aged and loved human beings? Shouldn't a humane, caring society—as ours is supposed to be—begin to consider ways to put my long-suffering mother, and the steadily growing number of miserable others like her, peacefully to sleep?"

Candidates for mercy killing

Otten suggests that ending a human life could be done with a pill, an injection, or other "quick means." He cautions that society should not consider this course of action for those whose minds are still alert or those who are comparatively well physically. But he says he is talking about the thousands of old men and women hopelessly crippled both in mind and body. These people are often kept alive with tube feeding, antibiotics, and other mechanical means.

Included in the list of people who could be considered candidates for mercy killing are those in comas, those who are paralyzed and begging to die, and others who are terminally ill and in pain.

For these people and those that Otten writes about, passive euthanasia may be an alternative. Passive euthanasia means to *let* someone die, to not take any measures to keep her alive, but also not to take any active measures, such as giving drugs to hasten her death. Basically, it means to do nothing. Since society does not condone going so far as to use a pill or injection, passive euthanasia can be accomplished by withholding food and water. "But why must it be done this slow, hard way?" asks Otten. He hopes that for people like his mother, a more humane method of helping someone die will be considered legal, moral, and ethical.

Reverend John Paris, a Jesuit priest, agrees that euthanasia may be justified. He says, "In our determination to prolong life at any cost, we have forgotten that dying is part of the process of living. These people's bodies are telling them there really is no purpose in going on, and yet we make them go on."

However, Frank Morriss, in *The Wanderer,* a Catholic newspaper, says euthanasia is never justified. He argues that if mercy killings were to become legal, people would become disposable. Furthermore, he questions the motives of those doing the killing. If a relative delivers a death-dealing pill to a dying man, is he doing it to end the man's suffering or because he can no longer face the burden of

"The artificial life support systems are intact, but I'd say Mr. Phipps could use a talking to."

caring for the ill person? Or worse, is the relative doing it because he stands to inherit a fortune upon the man's death?

A solution might be to allow only members of the medical community to make the euthanasia decision. But there are reservations about this also. If it is the doctor who practices active euthanasia, will it be done so matter-of-factly that she schedules it as she does any other nonemergency procedure, for say, next Wednesday, at 3:15?

Otten does not believe that this would happen. He thinks doctors would "surely be able to work out the best possible techniques for making so sensitive a decision."

Mercy killing and the courts

Occasionally we read in the newspaper of a mercy killing having taken place. So far society has taken a compassionate position toward such action. The courts, however, have been divided when it comes to judging who is guilty and must be punished, and who is justified in taking the action and does not have to go to prison. In one case where a suspended sentence was given, the court took into consideration the fact that there was no doubt the person wanted to die. She had tried more than once to commit suicide.

When active euthanasia has been practiced, the question often arises, Did the dying person *want* to die at this time? The answer will probably affect the outcome of an ensuing trial, as will another question, Was he or she capable of making that decision?

Going a step further, does every person have a right to decide when and how he or she will die?

The right to die—a living will

In a recent Harris Poll, 85 percent of those who responded favored patients having the right to tell the doctors to stop trying to extend their lives. They do not want to "live like vegetables," lying for weeks, even months, with tubes and oxygen tents sustaining a life that no longer has any meaning.

Those who feel strongly about this can declare while they are still competent what kind of medical treatment they desire. This kind of document is called a living will. It furnishes guidance to the physician, hospital, and family as to the wishes of the patient. It also provides a safeguard against family disagreements and wrenching deathbed decisions. If a living will has been made, the doctor and family know what treatment the patient wants and when to stop that treatment.

A living will helps eliminate lawsuits stemming from cases in which a hospital or doctor did not agree with a patient's wishes and kept him alive against his will. Some people in a comatose state have been kept alive for years.

A living will must be signed in the presence of two witnesses or a notary public. The witnesses should be people who do not stand to gain from the patient's death—a safeguard against the motive of inheritance, for example, that worries Frank Morriss and others. When making a living will, a person can be as specific as he likes. Usually a patient requests medication or medical procedures to provide comfort and to alleviate pain. If he wants to be tubefed, he can say so. He can state whether he will accept experimental drugs if their use will further medical knowledge. Or, conversely, he can state that he is opposed to this.

Another part of the living will may state where the patient wants to spend his last days—in a hospital, a hospice, or at home.

Dangerous documents

Those who are opposed to living wills believe such a document is not necessary and may even be dangerous. Luke Wilson, in an article in *The Right to Life of Michigan News*, thinks that living wills may not be fair to the elderly. He fears that "there is a real danger that all the hype today about 'living wills' is sending a not-so-subtle message to the sick and elderly. A message that they do have a 'duty to die' and let the rest of us get on with living."

People who agree with Wilson say that competent patients already

To My Family, My Physician, My Lawyer and All Others Whom It May Concern

Death is as much a reality as birth, growth, maturity and old age—it is the one certainty of life. If the time comes when I can no longer take part in decisions for my own future, let this statement stand as an expression of my wishes and directions, while I am still of sound mind.

If at such a time the situation should arise in which there is no reasonable expectation of my recovery from extreme physical or mental disability, I direct that I be allowed to die and not be kept alive by medications, artificial means or "heroic measures". I do, however, ask that medication be mercifully administered to me to alleviate suffering even though this may shorten my remaining life.

This statement is made after careful consideration and is in accordance with my strong convictions and beliefs. I want the wishes and directions here expressed carried out to the extent permitted by law. Insofar as they are not legally enforceable, I hope that those to whom this Will is addressed will regard themselves as morally bound by these provisions.

Signed _____

Date _____

Witness _____

Witness _____

Copies of this request have been given to _____

_____

_____

have the right to refuse medical treatment. If the wishes stated in a living will are followed, it may cut the family members out of their traditional role of making decisions for the dying person when he is no longer able to state his wishes.

However, this may be exactly why thousands of the elderly support the living will concept. They do not want their Uncle George or Cousin Susie to have the power to prolong their lives—or to cut their lives short.

Issues such as this bring up other questions. Who should make decisions about life and death—the individual, the family, the doctor, or the state (the courts)?

Infant euthanasia

Throughout recorded history, and no doubt earlier, babies with birth defects have been killed or left to die. Today this practice is called infant euthanasia. It is practiced in rare cases. The problems caused by this practice are similar to those encountered in any case where euthanasia is considered.

In his book *Endings*, Buff Bradley tells of a situation in which a doctor delivered a baby "so hideously deformed that to look upon it made the nurses turn away." The doctor left the baby alone on a table in the delivery room. It died within an hour. The doctor did nothing to keep the child alive. No tubes, no machines. He did not ask the parents' consent because he could not bring himself to show them their baby.

In another case, described by B.D. Colen, science editor of *Newsday* magazine, a severely deformed baby was taken home by her parents because it was not allowed to die. The infant, named Cara, had "a skull that looks as though it had been sawed off about two inches above [the] eyelids that are fused shut." Other parts of her body were deformed also. Colen says, "From the moment of her birth Cara was a candidate for infanticide. . . .In fact, what is surprising is not that she might have been killed, but that she was not."

A year and a half after her birth Cara was still being cared for by her parents at tremendous cost. The bandages on her head had to be changed every two hours at a cost of six hundred dollars a month. This and other expenses caused the family to ask the government to help pay for Cara's care. According to Colen, "Federal and state taxpayers are paying well over forty-three thousand dollars a year to maintain the life of a child who has no self-awareness, let alone an ability to receive and return love." When Cara dies, her mother says, it will be sad, "and it will be a great relief."

As medical skill and technology have developed to the point where infants with major defects can be saved, parents and physicians have been forced for the first time to confront difficult choices. Should they save severely deformed newborns?

Living forever: cryonics

Medical science has come a long way in the last hundred years. Advances continue to be made. What if doctors finally conquered death? If you could live forever, would you want to? Pondering the possibilities of a world where death is unknown is an interesting exercise for the imagination.

Stanley Klein, in his book *The Final Mystery*, discusses what that might be like:

Bloom County / By Berke Breathed

Try to imagine your own life in a world where no one ever dies. In such a world you would have a chance to meet people you have read about in history books. You might discover that you had some interesting ancestors. You would have many to choose from: two parents, four grandparents, eight great-grandparents, sixteen great-great-grandparents, thirty-two great-great-great-grandparents, and so on. If you kept counting backward, you would have to keep doubling the number of your ancestors.

This imaginary world might be interesting, at least for a while, but it probably would also be very crowded. Most of the earth's space would be taken up by places for all the people to live. Many, many people would have to live in each house. Even if only relatives had to live together, you might find yourself sharing your room with 1,024 great-great-great-great-great-great-great-great-grandmothers.

If you could stand the crowding, you might grow up and have children of your own. They would have to live in the same house

A technician opens a cryogenic storage capsule containing two frozen people at the Trans-Time Warehouse in Oakland, California. Cryogenics is the latest attempt by humans to cheat death.

too, along with the children of your brothers and sisters and of your thousands and thousands of cousins.

Finally, there would be no room on earth for more people. Governments probably would not permit any more babies to be born. People already living would just get older and older and older. . . . As sad as people may feel at the death of a friend, or how they may feel at the thought of their own death, they aren't all sure how good it would be to win the war against death. A world without death, and so, after a while, without new life, seems unnatural.

Even though Klein and others who have considered such a world find it undesirable, some people with incurable diseases will go to almost any lengths to win their battle with death. When they die, they want their bodies frozen. They hope that they can be brought back to life at some future time when a cure for their disease has been developed.

This means of suspending life is called cryonics. It promises eternal life—if it works. The body is chilled immediately upon death, or even before, and its blood is replaced with fluids that help prevent ice formation. It is a little like flushing a car's radiator and refilling it with antifreeze for a long winter. This process takes about twelve hours. Then the body's temperature is lowered to minus 110 degrees Fahrenheit by submersing it in isopropyl alcohol and dry ice. The body is then wrapped in insulation and placed upside down in a steel capsule filled with minus-320 degree liquid nitrogen. The feet are placed in the uppermost position as a safety precaution against leaks in the capsule. If the nitrogen level drops, the person's brain will be the last part to thaw.

Will it work?

The basic problem is that no one knows how to restore the body to life—yet.

However, the Alcor Life Extension Foundation of Riverside, California, will care for an entire body for one hundred thousand dollars, preserving it until the day comes when it is possible to revive it. This amount covers the freezing procedure, storage and handling, plus continuing maintenance and liquid nitrogen refills. If this seems too expensive, a head can be frozen for thirty-five thousand dollars and saved for the time when a cloned body might be grown and the head transplanted onto it.

Frozen cats and dogs

Some "cryonauts" have had their cats and dogs frozen along with their bodies. In this way they will be insured of companionship when they wake up centuries in the future when all their friends are gone.

Cryonics may sound like science fiction, but already certain whole body parts—especially small, tough ones such as arteries and bones—can be frozen and used in transplant surgery.

This new field of science opens up many possibilities—and creates some concerns. For instance, those who believe all humans have souls ask where the soul goes while the body is on ice. A spokesperson for a Roman Catholic archdiocese said it all depends on whether frozen bodies can be brought back to life. "The soul is that which gives humans life. So if they are capable of being brought back, the soul remains in the body. If not, the soul is entrusted to God."

In a field so new, most people have not yet formed clear-cut arguments for or against the desirability of "living forever."

CHAPTER SIX

Some Final Thoughts— Giving Meaning to Life and Death

In a children's book called *The Fall of Freddie the Leaf*, by Leo J. Buscaglia, Freddie watches as other leaves wither, die, and fall from the tree. He is afraid. He asks, "Will we all die?"

Daniel, an older and wiser leaf, answers, "Yes, everything dies. No matter how big or small, how weak or strong."

"But what is the purpose of it all?" asks Freddie.

Daniel thinks for a while. Then he says that giving shade to weary travelers is one good reason for a leaf to have been alive. Freddie finds some comfort in this and eventually comes to accept the fact of death. With his acceptance comes a kind of peace.

People, too, need to find a purpose to life in order to accept death and come to terms with it. When we accept death as a reality we can think about it matter-of-factly, talk about it, and even plan for it.

Finding a purpose to life

Elisabeth Kübler-Ross says, "Death is the final stage of growth in this life." She adds, "What is important is to realize that whether we understand fully why we are here . . .it is our purpose as human beings to grow—to look within ourselves to find and build upon that source of peace and understanding and strength which is our inner selves.''

Each person then must find his or her own purpose or meaning for life. How can this be done?

Author Joanne E. Bernstein suggests:

> Every so often, it's helpful to ask yourself what you would do if you only had one year to live. The responses you give define your concept of a full, meaningful life. If you ask the question now and then, you are likely to act upon some of your thoughts, even though you are well. It's a way to recognize your real goals and priorities and make plans to pursue some of them.

Dr. Robert A. Raab, who wrote *Coping with Death*, also believes that ''Constructive action [is what] makes life worthwhile.'' He says, ''We do not measure the worth of a book by the number of pages; nor do we measure a life by the number of years we have. . . . A shorter life, lived fully, can be more enriching than a long life without purpose and meaning.''

Some people find purpose and meaning in their accomplishments. One of these is tennis great Billie Jean King.

Leaving a legacy

King, who holds twenty Wimbledon tennis titles, was instrumental in founding the Women's Sports Foundation in 1974. In 1989 she is working on a recreational/competitive team approach to tennis. The teams are for men and women from under ten years of age to over eighty.

King believes that once the team tennis idea catches on it will be the most significant contribution she will have made in her life. Certainly Billie Jean King's name and accomplishments will be remembered. But not everyone is famous or is achieving such goals.

Some people leave memories that are a precious legacy. In an article in the *Minneapolis Star/Tribune* newspaper, Cynthia Vann tells why she will remember her fishing partner, Hawthorn.

I fish with a partner. His name is Hawthorn, and he's the one who frets over and sees to the fishing pole, bait, the attendant claptrap. . . . Hawthorn is 83 years old, and I met him on my first day on the lake. . . .

Hawthorn taught me how to make coffee in a skillet on an open fire, how to grow roses in dirt that is always damp, how to play gin rummy, how to get energy, he calls it, by lying on the granite rocks in the dawn. . . . He taught me how to fish. I love that old man. I could fish my way to the midst of infinity with Hawthorn, but of course the time will come when he can't make the day with me. When it happens, I'll manage as best I can. I have promised him I will.

Hawthorn told me to look at death. "Look it in the eye," he said, "and bear in mind there ain't a thing you can do about it." Hawthorn is a master of sane and obvious advice.

There is no doubt that Hawthorn has left a wonderful legacy to his friend. Most people who have thought about dying hope—even plan—to leave behind some sort of legacy, whether it is in the form of memories or something more tangible. An artist leaves paintings, a businessperson a bank account, an old lady her silver teapot. No

Two men console each other during a long walk. Seeking solitude and time to think about and feel deeply the mystery of life and death can deepen the meaning of our lives.

matter how large or small, material things may be valuable to those to whom they are left.

So that belongings will go to the person for whom they are intended, lawyers recommend writing a will.

Wills and life insurance

Joshua Rubenstein, an estate lawyer and partner in a New York law firm says, "Prepare a will as early as possible; for some, it may be advisable to do so as soon as you reach adulthood. If you die without a will, the chances are high that your property, however humble, will not end up in the hands of those you prefer."

A will does not have to be complicated. A handwritten letter lets others know what the deceased's wishes were. This may not have the legal weight that a will made out by a lawyer does, but it can serve a special purpose. One terminally ill man left a letter to his five-month-old grandson telling him about the best fishing holes near his lake cabin. Some people are better able to accept death when they know someone else will carry on family traditions.

Another way of leaving something tangible behind is to take out life insurance. Allstate Insurance Company explains, "A life insurance policy is a written contract between you and an insurance company. The contract is a promise to you, that if [when] you die, the insurance company will pay a designated amount of money to a person you name as your beneficiary, as long as your policy is in force." This means that if a person pays premiums (regular payments) for a specific period of time, her survivors will get a certain amount of money at the time of her death. The money from life insurance automatically goes to those named as beneficiaries, whether or not there is a will.

A legacy is a gift. Webster's dictionary says it is a "gift by will." The last (and perhaps the most valuable) gift people can give is to donate their organs to benefit the living. This can be done by filling out a donor form giving permission to have one's vital organs transplanted to another human being.

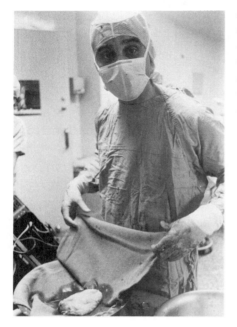

Dr. John Pennock, chief heart transplant surgeon at the Hershey Medical Center in Pennsylvania, displays a heart donated just minutes before. Donated organs can save the lives of others who need them.

An article in *The Wall Street Journal*, April 22, 1988, told of the desperate shortage of organs and tissues available for transplants. This shortage of organs can be relieved if more people donate their organs for transplantation surgery.

Many times organs are not made available because of old ideas that the body should not be tampered with, or because a doctor feels reluctant to approach a family about donation at the time of a death. It is easier for everyone if the dead person has expressed a wish that vital organs be donated if he or she dies in an accident.

The *Journal* article stated that "Two-thirds (66%) of the general public say they would be very likely to honor a family member's request to donate." If the family is not asked to allow the organs to be removed, they may be robbed of "what may be the one comfort available during a traumatic time."

An example of a family finding such comfort was the subject of a Dear Abby column in February 1989. James, a thirty-two-year-old man, had been seriously injured in a motorcycle accident. Brain activity had stopped, and the doctors said death was imminent. "It was James's wish," wrote his parents, "that after his death all usable organs should be harvested to help the living."

One of James's kidneys went to a thirty-five-year-old woman who was engaged to be married. She had been on a dialysis machine for five years. The other kidney went to a thirty-year-old married man with a family. James's heart went to a forty-three-year-old man whose own heart was rapidly failing. James's eyes were also used.

In some states persons are asked if they would be willing to donate their vital organs in case of accident when applying for their driver's license. It is something to think about.

Memories, money, property, fishing holes, and organs for transplantation are only some of the legacies left behind when people die. They are ways people try to live on in some way, for the wish for immortality is a universal wish.

Elisabeth Kübler-Ross explains that, "In order to be at peace [with death] it is necessary to feel a sense of history—that you are both part of what has come before and part of what is yet to come." Legacies give a meaning to life—and to death.

This does not mean that accepting death is easy.

Accepting the fact of death

People continue to turn away from even the mention of death, using words such as "he passed away," to soften the reality of this final mystery. Medical professionals continue to try to formulate an exact definition of death, and search for ways to delay it. Safety experts give us warnings and suggestions to prevent us from dying before our natural life spans are over. So, in many ways, people do face the fact that death is a reality.

Even though we don't like to think about it, death is going to happen. And would we want it otherwise?

"Would you want to live forever?" asks a character in *A House Like a Lotus*, by Madeleine L'Engle. Would you want "to go on in a body growing older and older, forever? Even if we could keep the body in reasonable shape, would you want to live forever?"

"Yes," his companion answers. Then, "No. Forever would be crippling. One would never have to do anything, because one could always do it tomorrow."

Dr. Robert A. Raab, in *Coping With Death*, quotes a similar thought in a phrase from an unknown philosopher: "Live every day as if it will be your last day on earth." Raab believes that stated this way, such a philosophy puts undue pressure on people. One must balance thoughts of life and death even though, "Each day of your life, something pertaining to death will present itself . . .death has a place in the scheme of human experience . . .[but] death should not dominate life."

To develop a philosophy of life and death, one most think about feelings, goals, and legacies. To do so, we may talk about death, read about it, and seek the wisdom to deal with it. Each person must develop his or her own philosophy.

Words written by others who have given much thought to the meaning of life and death can help. The following words were written by Henry Wadsworth Longfellow:

> Lives of great men all remind us
>   We can make our lives sublime,
> And, departing, leave behind us
>   Footprints on the sands of time . . .
>
>   Henry Wadsworth Longfellow
>   From *A Psalm of Life*

Suggestions for Further Reading

Fiction

Natalie Babbitt, *Tuck Everlasting*. New York: Farrar, Straus, & Giroux, 1975.

Marion Dane Bauer, *On My Honor*. New York: Clarion, 1986.

Margaret Wise Brown, *The Dead Bird*. New York: Dell, 1979.

Leo Buscaglia, *The Fall of Freddie the Leaf*. New York: Holt, Rinehart, & Winston, 1982.

Patricia Calvert, *The Hour of the Wolf*. New York: Signet, 1983.

Patricia Calvert, *The Stone Pony*. New York: Charles Scribner's Sons, 1982.

Lois Duncan, *I Know What You Did Last Summer*. New York: Little, Brown, 1973.

Mavis Jukes, *Blackberries in the Dark*. New York: Dell, 1987.

Marit Kaldhol, *Goodbye Rune*. (Trans. from Norwegian) New York: Kane Miller, 1987.

Madeleine L'Engle, *A House Like a Lotus*. New York: Dell, 1984.

Jane Resh Thomas, *Saying Good-bye to Grandma*. New York: Clarion, 1988.

Judith Viorst, *The Tenth Good Thing About Barney*. New York: Macmillan, 1971.

Charlotte Zolotow, *My Grandson Lew*. New York: Harper & Row, 1985.

Nonfiction

Caroline Arnold, *What We Do When Someone Dies*. New York: Franklin Watts, 1987.

David L. Bender, ed., et at., *Death/Dying: Opposing Viewpoints Sources*, St. Paul, MN: Greenhaven Press, Inc. 1985.

Joanne E. Bernstein, *Loss and How to Cope with it*. New York: Seabury Press, 1977.

Buff Bradley, *Endings*. Reading, MA: Addison-Wesley, 1979.

David Carroll, *Living with Dying*. New York: McGraw-Hill, 1985.

Judith E. Greenberg and Helen H. Carey, *Sunny: The Death of a Pet*. New York: Franklin Watts, 1986.

Earl A. Grollman, *Living When a Loved One Has Died*. Boston: Beacon Press, 1977.

Sharon Grollman, *Shira: A Legacy of Courage*. New York: Doubleday, 1988.

Stanley Klein, *The Final Mystery*. Garden City, NY: Doubleday and Company, 1974.

Jill Krementz, *How It Feels When a Parent Dies*. New York: Alfred A. Knopf, 1981.

Elisabeth Kübler-Ross, *On Children and Death*. New York: Macmillan Publishing Co., 1983.

Elisabeth Kübler-Ross, *Questions and Answers on Death and Dying*. New York: Macmillan Publishing Co., 1974

Elisabeth Kübler-Ross, *To Live Until We Say Good-bye*. Englewood Cliffs, NJ: Prentice-Hall, Inc., 1978.

Elaine Landau, *Alzheimer's Disease*. New York: Franklin Watts, 1987.

Jane Mersky Leder, *Dead Serious: A Book for Teenagers About Teenage Suicide*. New York: Atheneum, 1987.

Astrid Lindgren, *The Brothers Lionheart*. New York: The Viking Press, 1973.

Kim Long and Terry Reim, *Kicking the Bucket*. New York: William Morrow, 1985.

Mary McHugh, *Young People Talk About Death*. New York: Franklin Watts, 1980.

Lisa Ann Marsoli, *Things to Know About Death and Dying*. Morristown, NJ: Silver Burdett Company, 1985.

Jessica Mitford, *The American Way of Death*. New York: Fawcett Crest, 1963.

Herbert A. Nieburg and Arlene Fischer, *Pet Loss*. New York: Harper & Row, 1982.

Steve Olson and Owen B. Toon, "The Warm Earth," *Science*, 1985.

Robert A. Raab, *Coping with Death*. New York: The Rosen Publishing Group, Inc., 1983.

Janelle Rohr, ed., *Death and Dying*. St. Paul, MN: Greenhaven Press, Inc., 1987.

Norma Simon, *The Saddest Time*. Niles, IL: A. Whitman, 1986.

Judie Smith, *Coping with Suicide*. New York: The Rosen Publishing Group, Inc., 1986.

The Unit at Fayerweather Street School, Eric E. Rofes, ed., *The Kids' Book About Death and Dying*. Boston: Little, Brown and Company, 1985.

Yvonne Williams, "Just for Kids," *Bereavement*, January, 1989.

Index

Picture Credits

About the Author

Norma Gaffron is a former school teacher who lives in New Brighton, Minnesota. She has been a professional writer for the past eleven years. Her articles, on topics as diverse as sailing, snakes, and replanting lost teeth, have appeared in many national magazines. She has been a Junior Great Books leader and is regional advisor for the National Society of Children's Books. *Dealing with Death* is Ms. Gaffron's first book in the Overview Series.